Carol Read's 101 Tips for Teaching Primary Children

Cambridge Handbooks for Language Teachers

This series, now with over 50 titles, offers practical ideas, techniques and activities for the teaching of English and other languages, providing inspiration for both teachers and trainers.

The Pocket Editions come in a handy, pocket-sized format and are crammed full of tips and ideas from experienced English language teaching professionals, to enrich your teaching practice.

Recent titles in this series:

Classroom Management Techniques
JIM SCRIVENER

Translation and Own-language Activities
PHILIP KERR

Language Learning with Digital Video
BEN GOLDSTEIN AND PAUL DRIVER

Discussions and More
Oral fluency practice in the classroom
PENNY UR

Interaction Online
Creative Activities for Blended Learning
LINDSAY CLANDFIELD AND JILL HADFIELD

Activities for Very Young Learners
HERBERT PUCHTA AND KAREN ELLIOTT

Teaching and Developing Reading Skills
PETER WATKINS

Lexical Grammar
Activities for teaching chunks and exploring patterns
LEO SELIVAN

Off the Page
Activities to bring lessons alive and enhance learning
CRAIG THAINE

Teaching in Challenging Circumstances
CHRIS SOWTON

Recent Pocket Editions:

Penny Ur's 100 Teaching Tips
PENNY UR

Jack C. Richards' 50 Tips for Teacher Development
JACK C. RICHARDS

Scott Thornbury's 30 Language Teaching Methods
SCOTT THORNBURY

Alan Maley's 50 Creative Activities
ALAN MALEY

Scott Thornbury's 101 Grammar Questions
SCOTT THORNBURY

Mark Hancock's 50 Tips for Teaching Pronunciation
MARK HANCOCK

David Crystal's 50 Questions About English Usage
DAVID CRYSTAL

Herbert Puchta's 101 Tips for Teaching Teenagers
HERBERT PUCHTA

Carol Read's 101 Tips for Teaching Primary Children

Carol Read

Consultant and editor: Scott Thornbury

CAMBRIDGE
UNIVERSITY PRESS

University Printing House, Cambridge CB2 8BS, United Kingdom

One Liberty Plaza, 20th Floor, New York, NY 10006, USA

477 Williamstown Road, Port Melbourne, VIC 3207, Australia

314–321, 3rd Floor, Plot 3, Splendor Forum, Jasola District Centre,
New Delhi – 110025, India

103 Penang Road, #05-06/07, Visioncrest Commercial, Singapore 238467

Cambridge University Press is part of the University of Cambridge.

It furthers the University's mission by disseminating knowledge in the pursuit of
education, learning and research at the highest international levels of excellence.

www.cambridge.org
Information on this title: www.cambridge.org/9781108744225

First published 2020

20 19 18 17 16 15 14 13 12 11 10 9 8 7 6 5

Printed in Great Britain by CPI Group (UK) Ltd, Croydon CR0 4YY

A catalogue record for this publication is available from the British Library

ISBN 978-1-108-74422-5 Paperback
ISBN 978-1-108-74425-6 Apple iBook
ISBN 978-1-108-74424-9 Google eBook
ISBN 978-1-108-74423-2 Kindle eBook
ISBN 978-1-108-74421-8 ebooks.com eBook

Contents

Acknowledgements

The authors and publishers acknowledge the following sources of copyright material and are grateful for the permissions granted. While every effort has been made, it has not always been possible to identify the sources of all the material used, or to trace all copyright holders. If any omissions are brought to our notice, we will be happy to include the appropriate acknowledgements on reprinting and in the next update to the digital edition, as applicable.

Text

Tip 99: Story review. Copyright © James Matthews.

Thanks

Special thanks to Karen Momber and Scott Thornbury for inviting me to write this book and to Scott for his positive and helpful feedback on the draft. Huge thanks also to Alison Sharpe for her meticulous and insightful editing skills and for being such a pleasure to work with, and to Jo Timerick for her help behind the scenes. Thanks, as ever, to my husband, Alan Matthews, for his personal support and to all the teachers and children I've worked with over so many years from whom I've learnt so much.

Dedication

For every primary language teacher who strives to develop a love of learning in every child.

Why I wrote this book

There are many more children than adults learning English as a foreign language in classrooms around the world. And yet English language teaching to adults is often perceived as the default and, until quite recently, has led the way in areas such as teacher education, classroom methodology and research.

I hope that the tips in this book will help to unpack the range of knowledge, skills, attitudes and professional qualities that are needed to teach children and contribute to creating a new, **age-appropriate** default. In writing the tips, I have drawn, above all, on my experience as a classroom practitioner in different contexts, mainly in Europe and Latin America, over many years. I have also drawn on reading and research which has contributed to knowledge and understanding of primary English language teaching globally. My experience as a parent, and as a teacher educator, working with primary teachers and trainers in many countries all over the world, has also influenced my perspective.

At the heart of the tips is a belief that, in order to be effective, you need to master basic skills and techniques that enable you to positively embrace the challenges of working with lively, diverse classes of children. At the same time, and above all, you need to see your role as an educator of children. This means adopting an approach in which you continually take into account all aspects of children's social, emotional, psychological, physical and **cognitive development** as an integral part of your teaching, rather than narrowly focusing on language learning **outcomes** alone.

The tips in this book are designed to cover the years that children are in primary education, approximately aged six to twelve, and reference is made to lower and upper primary when relevant. However, as the educational approach, language background, literacy development, age and maturity of children vary in different cultural contexts, you are the best judge to decide which tips are appropriate to implement with which age groups in your situation.

The most helpful and rewarding way to use this book may be to start with a topic or tip that particularly interests you and move around from there. Referencing between tips is included to guide you in making connections to related themes. References to specific ideas or books mentioned in the tips are provided at the bottom of each page. The glossary on page 128 also provides an explanation of key terminology used.

Although the book is primarily directed at primary language teachers of English, the same principles and tips can be applied if you are teaching other modern, foreign languages. As a follow-up, in order to expand your understanding of theory which underpins some of the tips and get more ideas, I recommend that you read, or at least dip into, the Selected further reading listed on page 135.

Finally, I'm aware that everything in this book, from the choice of topics and content of the tips to the personal views expressed, derives from my own background, beliefs and experience as a primary language teacher in particular contexts. I therefore strongly encourage you to use your own personal and cultural filters, and to select and reflect critically, before applying or adapting the tips to your context.

Above all, I hope the book gives you food for thought and will be a useful guide in helping you to teach primary children with confidence and success.

A: Getting started

As the saying goes, you only have one chance to make a first impression. That's the same in all walks of life, including teaching primary children. As far as possible, you need to create an impression that will lay foundations for developing a harmonious working relationship as from the first lesson. This includes establishing your credibility as teacher, displaying relaxed confidence in your role, showing care and interest in relating to children personally, planning and delivering interesting and challenging lessons, noticing children's responses and listening to what they have to say. It also involves setting clear **parameters of behaviour** and ensuring that learning **outcomes** are relevant and worthwhile.

That's quite a tall order and, however much experience you have, it's natural to feel slightly nervous before teaching a class of primary children for the first time – at least I know I always do. In my experience, it helps when initial lessons lead to concrete learning outcomes which link learning to children's life outside the classroom. In the case of lower primary, this might be making a simple origami book (see **63**) with personal information that children take home to show and share with their families. With upper primary, it might be creating a personal blog (see **89**), with content of their choice, which they can subsequently add to in a regular way during the course.

My key tips for getting started are:
1 **Learn children's names – fast!**
2 **Keep it personal and encourage aspirations**
3 **Establish classroom routines**
4 **Start as you mean to continue**

1 Learn children's names – fast!

> By remembering and using children's names from the outset, you signal your interest in them as individuals. This boosts their self-esteem and makes them more likely to listen and actively engage in lessons.

When you start teaching a class for the first time, there are usually some children whose names you remember more easily than others. In order to avoid any perception of favouritism, it's important to make an effort to learn all the children's names as soon as you can.

For the first few lessons, it helps to make a plan of the classroom with the children's names and photos showing where they sit. You can keep this on your desk or computer screen and refer to it unobtrusively as you teach.

With younger children, you can prepare circular medallions of coloured card with the children's first names in marker pen and a hole at the top threaded with easily breakable wool. As you give out the medallions for children to wear, ask, *What's your name? / My name's ...* or *Who's ...? / I am!* in order to identify each child's medallion and give yourself an opportunity to learn their names.

Older children can make name cards by folding an A4 sheet in three equal sections, writing their names in the middle section, and drawing a logo to show a favourite possession or interest, e.g. a football or cat. At the start of the first few lessons, children stand their name cards on their desks.

In classes where children are together for the first time, you can also do activities to learn everyone's names. One example is where children stand in a circle in groups and take turns to say and then repeat each other's names cumulatively, following a simple, clapping rhythm. However, in contexts where children already know each other, there's little point in doing an activity like this. Instead, an activity where children work in groups and create a simple crossword with clues using their first names, and then exchange and do each other's crosswords or try them out on you, will be more appropriate.

Keep it personal and encourage aspirations   2

Children need to feel that you care about their personal lives and aspirations. This is motivating and helps to build positive relationships.

The more you know about children, the more you can relate to them individually and understand their needs and preferences (see also **5**). Every lesson offers opportunities for this, e.g. when you personalise a topic or ask children their views, but it is particularly important when you start working with a class for the first time.

One activity to find out personal interests is to get children to create their own coat of arms, divided into four sections. Children draw and/ or write in each section, either choosing from a range of options or following your instructions, e.g. their favourite free time activity, food, sport or school subject, their pet (or pet they would like to have) and a place they would like to visit. Children take turns to show their coat of arms and talk about their choices. These can also be displayed and used as the basis for other activities, e.g. *Who's got a hamster?* / *How many of you like basketball?* / *Find the coat of arms most similar to yours.*

An activity that encourages children to think about their aspirations for learning English is to make a dream tree. Create an outline of the trunk and branches of a tree. Give every child a piece of green paper in the shape of a leaf. Children write on the leaf one thing they want to achieve in English and stick it on the tree, e.g. *I want to watch Harry Potter films.* Children then share and compare their aspirations.

Finding out about children in this way allows you to make references to them naturally in subsequent lessons, e.g. *Did you take your dog for a walk at the weekend, Isabel?* / *Mario loves maths, so perhaps he can tell us.* This shows that you know and care about the children and heightens their **self-esteem**. You can also use their aspirations to inform your lesson planning (see **D**) and this is likely to lead to increased **engagement** too.

3   Establish classroom routines

> Classroom routines give a framework and structure to lessons. They make lesson preparation and classroom management easier and save valuable teaching time.

You can establish **classroom routines** in relation to any area of your teaching where you feel that it will be beneficial for children to follow a predictable pattern of behaviour. These are likely to include, among others, starting and ending lessons, getting attention, asking questions, giving out and collecting materials, working in pairs and groups (see **7**), reviewing learning (see **19**). Classroom routines need to be **age-appropriate**. With younger children, an opening classroom routine might include greetings and a hello song using a class puppet, followed by identifying the weather and day of the week. With older children, lessons might start with a high-five greeting and a hello rap, followed by brief 'news of the day' from children who choose to contribute.

In order to establish a classroom routine, you need to explain why the routine is important, use the routine regularly, **model** the behaviour you expect, and be persistent in expecting children to conform to this. For example, if you establish a routine whereby you use a tambourine or count down from five as a signal for children to stop whatever they're doing, listen and pay attention, resist the temptation to continue before you have the attention of the whole class.

Some classroom routines can be established collaboratively by negotiating a **class contract** with children. If children themselves agree on the value of classroom routines, such as raising hands to ask questions, then they are much more likely to keep to them.

Classroom routines make children feel secure and develop their **autonomy**. Through the use of regularly repeated, shared scenarios and language patterns, classroom routines also create a sense of class community and promote confidence and ownership of learning.

Start as you mean to continue

During the first few weeks when you meet a class, children are willing to respect you and accept the way you do things. This is a critical period for you to establish positive relationships and an agreed way of working. It is much harder to change things later on.

If you feel nervous meeting a class for the first time and are worried that this may have a negative impact, try the 'as if' technique. This involves acting 'as if' you are the most confident teacher in the world, using relaxed, open body language and a calmly projected voice. If you consciously stage act for the first few lessons, you're likely to find that the children's positive response will boost your confidence and help you become the teacher you wish to be.

In developing a positive working relationship (see **5**), it is a basic requirement to show genuine interest and respect for children and to learn their names (see **1**). You also need to give encouragement, support, **feedback** and praise as appropriate (see **11**). At the same time, you need to be firm in insisting on what you consider are acceptable **parameters of behaviour** so that these become a habit and classroom norm.

In order to establish an agreed way of working, it helps to have a clear vision of how you would ideally like things to be. You then need to plan in detail how to achieve this.

In addition to organising the environment, planning lessons and **classroom routines**, it is useful to prepare a **behaviour plan**. A behaviour plan gives you an opportunity to think through what you consider acceptable parameters of behaviour and the strategies you will use to get children to accept and respect these. A behaviour plan can include things such as (negotiated) classroom rules, a **reward system** (if you plan to use one), strategies for managing behaviour (see **12**), and consequences for inappropriate behaviour. Thinking these through in advance will help you to be consistent in the way you respond to children and to reach a shared understanding of how to work together.

B: Core skills

There are a number of core skills which will underpin your confidence in working with children and are essential to successful teaching and learning. These core skills relate to creating a positive rapport with your learners and thinking carefully about language you use in lessons. They also relate to selecting, setting up and managing activities in a way that maximises learning opportunities and supports your ability to deliver lessons in the most productive way.

For example, with an activity such as dictation, you may choose to do it either as a whole class activity (see **81**), or as pair work, using copies of the same text with different missing words which children dictate to their partner, or as group work, in which children take turns to dictate a text from the wall to their group. In making your choice, you need to weigh up the potential risks and benefits for skills development, **cooperative learning**, enjoyment and orderly classroom management (see **C**).

When you first start teaching children, you may find it useful to write a detailed script of language you are going to use to give instructions and stage-by-stage notes of how you plan to set up a pair or group work activity effectively. As you become more skilled and proficient in these areas, you'll find that you no longer need to do this, and these basic, pedagogical skills will become a natural and automatic part of your 'teaching persona' and performance.

My key tips for core skills are:
   5   **Build positive relationships**
   6   **Watch your language!**
   7   **Set up pair and group work effectively**
   8   **Choose and use activities wisely**

Build positive relationships   **5**

> Building positive relationships lies at the heart of effective primary teaching. As well as promoting participation, it also helps you to manage your classes in a positive way.

The way you relate to children, individually and collectively, and the way children relate to each other, has a fundamental influence on their **self-esteem**, attitudes, behaviour and achievement. Building positive relationships also links closely to **values** education (see **H**) since it is through the development of values such as trust, mutual respect, kindness, inclusion and cooperation, that strong, healthy relationships develop.

In order to build positive relationships, you need to:

- **Model** social skills you wish children to adopt, for example, saying 'please' and 'thank you', using eye contact and active listening.
- Use humour but never at any child's expense.
- Create an **inclusive** classroom by encouraging a team spirit and using inclusive language, such as *Let's … / We're going to …* (see also **69**).
- Find things in common by doing activities such as Cat or dog? Say pairs of related words, e.g. *Pizza or hamburger?* Children identify the item they prefer and share reasons for their choice.
- Make personal connections by doing activities such as Guess the lie! Children write three sentences about themselves, one of which is a lie. They take turns to say their sentences and guess the lie.
- Value children's **multilingual identities** (see **44**).
- Find moments for individual contact. Use these to show you care.
- Look for things to praise (rather than criticise) in relation to children's work, participation and behaviour (see also **11**).
- Include collective activities that create a sense of community, such as storytelling and singing (see **F** and **I**).
- Include **cooperative learning** activities that practise social skills as well as language (see, e.g. **G, J, 60, 66, 75**).

6 | Watch your language!

> The way you use language in class is crucial in assisting children's learning. It needs to be natural and provide input that children can understand and be closely matched to their cognitive and social development.

In pitching your language appropriately for lower primary children, it's helpful to adopt some features of the way parents typically interact with young children learning their mother tongue. These include repeating words and phrases frequently, asking questions to keep attention, expanding what children say and using simple, grammatical structures and slower, but not unnatural, articulation. They also include using gestures, actions and facial expression to support understanding, and responding to children's meaning by **recasting** and reformulating what they want to say, rather than overtly correcting them (see also **96**). As children get older and become more linguistically and cognitively proficient, you need to continually adapt and grade your language to their level.

Some key areas to think about in the way you use language include:

- Giving instructions: simplify these into stages and avoid complex grammatical constructions.
- **Think aloud** techniques: explicitly verbalise and **model** how to go about solving a problem or doing an activity.
- Eliciting techniques: use prompts, e.g. *And …? / So …?*, and questions, e.g. *Anything else?*, to gather children's suggestions, ideas and get them to display what they know.
- Checking comprehension: plan ways to get evidence of children's understanding. For example, rather than *Do you understand what a reptile is?* ask *Is a snake a reptile? How do you know?*
- Using the children's **shared language**: this may be appropriate at times, for example, for explanations or to check instructions (see also **44**).

Set up pair and group work effectively

> Pair and group work provide opportunities to maximise language practice and develop cooperative learning skills – but they also risk escalating noise levels and even losing control of the class. The secret lies in how you set up, manage and monitor activities.

In order to work effectively, you need to provide a clear framework and purpose for pair and group work. You need to indicate partners or groups (for example, children sitting next to, or behind, them) and give clearly staged instructions (see **6**). It's also vital to prepare language you expect children to use, for example, by getting them to practise this in chorus first. You also need to demonstrate or do the activity with the whole class before they begin, and give a signal for starting and stopping.

During pair and group work, you need to **monitor** closely, without interfering unless necessary, and have something ready for fast-finishers to do. It also helps to train children to use 'our quiet voices' (see **73**), to keep activities short at first, and to provide opportunities for reporting back, demonstrating the activity or doing a **learning review** (see **19**), at the end.

Pair work is easier to manage than group work and it is advisable to start with this. Examples of activities that lend themselves to pair work include games (see **G**), drama (see **Q**), and grammar practice (see **95**). As children get older, pair work is also useful for getting them to compare ideas and check answers in **think-pair-share** activities too (see **82**).

The key to successful group work lies in organising children effectively (see **9** and **15**) and ensuring that everyone has a role and is motivated to contribute. In some activities, such as **cumulative** games (see **82**) and wall dictations (see introduction to **B**), the design of the activity means that everyone contributes equally. For others, such as projects (see **J**) and presentations (see **60**), it may be useful to give specific roles, such as timekeeper, notetaker, content checker, reporter.

8 Choose and use activities wisely

> By choosing and using activities wisely, you can positively influence children's attitudes, behaviour and response. This supports your teaching and leads to more productive learning outcomes.

Any activity that you do in class impacts on children's attitudes, behaviour and response (see also **9**). A key skill is to recognise when different kinds of activities may be suitable.

If you wish to promote learner **autonomy** and responsible decision-making in relation to homework (providing you teach in a context where you can decide whether or not to set this), get children to brainstorm the pros and cons of homework in groups. Alternatively, give each group a list of pros and cons in jumbled order on strips of paper, and they sort them into two sets, e.g. pros: *It helps me learn more. / I learn at my own pace. / I learn how to manage my time. / I can ask mum or dad for help.* etc.; cons: *I don't have time. / It's boring. / I want to play. / It doesn't help me learn.* etc. Use the sorted statements as the basis for a discussion culminating in a class vote on whether to have homework or not. In my experience, children invariably decide that it is worth having some homework, even if only once a week or voluntarily. They then go on to decide the kind of homework they would like. By giving children **agency**, they feel empowered and are more likely to commit to the agreed **outcome** in a responsible way.

If you have a large class and are concerned about keeping control, you may feel that, at least at first, it is too risky to set up pair or group work and wiser to do whole class activities that progress in a **lockstep** way. These might include storytelling (see **F**), choral repetition (see **82**), flashcard games (see **55**), TPR activities (see **65**), dictations (see **81**) and whole class discussions (see **31**). In this case, you need to use your professional judgement in order to balance the value of achieving successful learning outcomes through being able to marshal children's attentional resources and maintain a degree of control versus a freer, more learner-centred approach.

C: Classroom management

Classroom management is the backbone of effective primary teaching. If you're not able to manage your class, nothing seems to go right. If your classroom management is effective, everything else seems to fall into place.

The main aim of classroom management with children is to create a happy, relaxed working atmosphere in which the norms and **parameters of behaviour** are respected. Children feel secure and supported by the teacher, at the same time as they are helped to become increasingly independent in the way they approach their learning.

I learnt my classroom management skills the hard way. I always remember a difficult moment years ago when I got a class of 40 ten-year-olds to do a communicative activity, which involved moving around the class to exchange information. Although the activity started well, things soon got out of control. From this early experience, I developed two personal maxims which have stood me in good stead ever since:

- Softly, softly: when introducing new techniques, proceed slowly, keep activities short and always give reasons for doing things that children understand.
- Stay serene: just as a raised, agitated voice tends to heighten the level of excitement and noise, outward calm, strong, open, relaxed body language and a quiet voice find reflection in the children's behaviour too.

My key tips for classroom management are:

 9 **Organisation is key**
10 **Adopt a positive approach**
11 **Use praise with care**
12 **Manage behaviour strategically**

Organisation is key

Classroom management is to do with organising all aspects of the learning environment. The more you plan, prepare and organise things in advance, the easier it becomes.

Here are 'seven pillars of organisation' that are basic to classroom management:

1 Organising the classroom: this relates principally to the arrangement of desks. If you have a choice, consider the pros and cons of different options, such as desks in rows, groups or a U-shape.

2 Organising the children: this involves whether children always sit in the same place and whether in random, friendship, ability or mixed ability groupings.

3 Organising activities: this relates to setting up and sequencing activities. It includes the principle of **stir and settle** so that lively activities are followed by quieter ones to calm children down (see also **8**).

4 Organising time: this involves organising a varied balance of activities, with extra ideas in case you have more time (see also **13**).

5 Organising resources: this relates to organising resources so that they are clearly labelled and easily retrievable. With homemade resources, e.g. sets of picture cards, you may wish to laminate these and number them so that they can be kept in sets and re-used (see also **78**).

6 Organising records: in most contexts, you need to keep a class register, a record of work done and a record of children's progress. This is important for accountability.

7 Organising yourself: this is vital! If, for example, you spend time searching for flashcards at the start of a lesson, this is likely to be when you lose the children's attention and may find it hard to regain.

MacLennan, S. (1987). 'Integrating lesson planning and class management', *ELT Journal* 41/3, 193–197.

Adopt a positive approach

> **Adopting a positive approach means using a model of influence, rather than a model of control, and actively planning ways to improve classroom management.**

It is a myth that you can control children's behaviour. There's only one person in the classroom whose behaviour you can control, and that's *you*. In order to positively influence children's behaviour, you need to look to your own behaviour first. For example, if you are calm and polite, this will influence the way children respond. If you signal for attention and wait for silence with relaxed, open body language, rather than showing irritation and raising your voice, children are more likely to comply.

A positive approach to classroom management includes being:

- proactive in setting up clear **parameters of behaviour** and anticipating likely problems in advance;
- reflective in regularly reviewing and implementing changes to make improvements;
- aware of the need to treat children as individuals and create a supportive **affective climate** for learning;
- strategic in helping children become responsible for their behaviour and showing that you value this;
- active in enhancing children's **self-esteem** and the sense of success this brings;
- positive in your expectations of children's behaviour and their ability to achieve, as they will invariably live up to these.

However, above all it means engaging your classes in lively, varied, suitably challenging lessons in which you make children feel valued and listen to what they have to say and show that you believe in what they can achieve.

11 Use praise with care

> Praise develops children's self-esteem and helps you manage behaviour. However, you need to use it carefully and in age-appropriate ways.

Praise makes children feel good, but it can produce other feelings as well. The least helpful praise is when you say, e.g. *That's a good story*, and pass judgement without saying why. This can create anxiety (*Does she mean it?*) and lead to a lack of confidence.

The most helpful praise is descriptive, e.g. *That's a good story. I notice that you've thought carefully about the beginning, middle and end.* This gives constructive **feedback** and guides children in building up positive self-beliefs about what they can do, and in learning to evaluate their own work (see **32** and **100**).

You can also use praise (always sincere, never fake) to manage children's behaviour. Examples are:

- Praise early on: if you make positive comments at the start of lessons, this makes children feel good about themselves and their learning and helps prevent inappropriate behaviour.
- Peripheral praise: if a child is **off-task**, move to where they are and praise another child nearby who is working well. Look at the child briefly to convey your message before moving away again.
- *By the way ...* : say, e.g. *By the way, well done for waiting your turn.* This shows that you notice and value the way children behave but without making an issue of it.

In lower primary, praise provides instant feedback and encouragement to participate. However, as children get older, you need to use praise more discriminatingly. You also need to consider whether to praise publicly or in private as pre-adolescent children may feel uncomfortable getting praise from the teacher in front of their peers.

Manage behaviour strategically

> **Although responding to children's behaviour can be challenging, it helps to prepare strategies in advance.**

Three things that have helped me are:

1   Catch them being good (CBG). Look for what children are doing right and acknowledge it (see also **11**). By doing this consistently, you give the message that it is appropriate behaviour that gets your attention and that you value this as much as children's work.

2   Use the criterion of whether children's behaviour is actually stopping you from teaching, and children from learning, to decide if and how you'll intervene. Try the ABCD strategy where A = Appropriate (or Angelic) behaviour (i.e. **on task**); B = Boring But Bearable (**off task** but not disruptive); C = Caution. Handle with Care. D = Disruptive or Dangerous. Aim to intervene minimally and avoid confrontation. If you tell a child off about a B level of behaviour, e.g. kicking legs annoyingly under the desk, even though the behaviour is not stopping you from teaching or other children from learning, you risk confrontation and escalating the level of behaviour to C or D.

3   When you need to intervene, move from taking low-key to more forceful action as necessary. Some options are:

- Tactical ignoring: when you decide not to pay any attention to the behaviour, and that alone stops it.
- Non-verbal signal: when you use gesture, eye contact, or move nearer the child.
- Verbal signal: when you name a child parenthetically as you speak, e.g. *So we're going to work in pairs – Dani, legs on the floor, please.*
- Instruction: when you say, e.g. *Listen now, please!* (not *Don't talk now!* which makes children think of talking and is least effective).
- Directed choice: when you ask, e.g. *Would you like to start work now or stay in at break time?*
- Command: when you say, e.g. *Alex, get down off the window sill now!* in a voice that shows you expect immediate compliance.

D: Lesson planning

Lesson planning can make the whole difference between a great lesson and a disaster. The more prepared you are, the more confident and relaxed you feel in class. Having a clear lesson plan also frees you up to be able to respond more spontaneously to children, and to deal more effectively with all the on-the-spot micro-management moments and decisions that arise in any lesson.

Metaphors are often helpful in exploring aspects of teaching and learning. In many ways, a lesson plan for teaching is like a recipe for cooking. With a recipe, you have a clear idea of the culinary result you are aiming for. With a lesson plan, you also need to have a clear idea of the learning **outcomes** that you wish to achieve. Both recipes and lesson plans also have a variety and balance of ingredients. In a recipe, the ingredients vary in quantity, texture, colour and flavour. In a lesson plan, they vary in materials, activity types, skills and interaction patterns. Both recipes and lesson plans include a method with clear stages and timing to produce a successful result. However, there's also room for creative adaptation and, depending on your confidence and experience, you can improvise freely.

When you start out, either cooking or teaching, it's usually a good idea to follow a detailed recipe or lesson plan as your principal guide. As you become more proficient, however, you may find that following certain procedures becomes so much part of your automatic, internalised behaviour that you no longer need to rely on quite so much detail.

My key tips for lesson planning are:

13 **Plan in sand, not stone!**

14 **Focus on learning outcomes and success criteria**

15 **Aim for variety and balance**

16 **Plan in learning cycles**

Plan in sand, not stone!

> However much experience you have, you can never predict exactly how a lesson will go. For this reason, you always need to build flexibility into your lesson plan.

Lessons do not always go to plan. Activities may take more, or less, time than you had anticipated, and children may respond more, or less, enthusiastically to what you get them to do. Whatever the reasons for this, your first responsibility is to respond to the needs of the children rather than sticking rigidly to your lesson plan, and you need to have contingency plans in place to deal with this. Such plans involve identifying stages or activities in advance from your lesson that can be omitted if need be. They also involve having additional material ready in case children need extension activities or extra support in carrying out planned activities, or you get through everything in your lesson plan faster than you'd expected.

If you find you don't have time for all the activities in your lesson plan, don't be tempted to rush through everything. It's much better to leave time to bring the lesson to a close and do a **learning review** in your usual way (see **19**). You can always move the activities you didn't have time for into your next lesson.

There are also times when it may be appropriate to abandon your lesson plan altogether. One occasion I vividly remember was while teaching a unit of work on bugs to lower primary children. The children loved the topic and one lesson a child proudly turned up with a shoebox full of silkworms munching on mulberry leaves. The rest of the class were so intrigued that I decided to abandon my lesson plan and we spent the next hour finding out about and observing the silkworms: counting them, drawing them, inventing a song (*One little, two little, three little silkworms …*) and describing them by building up a co-constructed text on the board (see **85**). The benefits of this spontaneous decision, in terms of the children's **engagement** and obvious enthusiasm to learn, more than made up for the *ad hoc* nature of the plan.

14 Focus on learning outcomes and success criteria

> Learning outcomes and success criteria give a framework and purpose to your lesson. When you share or co-construct success criteria with children, this impacts positively on their learning too.

Learning **outcomes** specify what children will be able to do by the end of the lesson. For example, *By the end of the lesson, children will know ... / be able to ... / understand that ... / be aware of ...* . Learning outcomes are best explained in a child-friendly way at the start of the lesson, including their purpose and relevance, and using the children's mother tongue or **shared language** if need be. It may also be helpful to note learning outcomes in bullet points on the board. They can then be referred to during the lesson and reviewed at the end.

Success criteria answer the question: *How will you know that the learning outcome has been achieved?* They constitute a checklist of features that demonstrate that children have achieved the learning outcome successfully. For example, a learning outcome might be *By the end of the lesson, children will be able to write a short personal description.* Success criteria might include: *Write your name and age. / Write where you live. / Describe your family. / Write free time activities you like and don't like. / Use full stops and capital letters. / Join sentences using 'and' or 'but'.*

By sharing success criteria with children, you make learning goals tangible and explicit. Children have a clear focus for their work and know what they need to do. This encourages them to be more independent and take greater responsibility for their learning. It also helps them to evaluate their progress, identify difficulties and consider how they might improve (see also **99** and **100**).

It is often particularly motivating when you co-construct success criteria with children. For example, if the learning outcome is to produce a fact file about an endangered animal, ask children: *What do we need to include in our fact file to be successful?* Listen and guide their ideas as necessary. The list you create together raises children's awareness of features to include in their work and gives them ownership of the task as well.

Aim for variety and balance **15**

> Lessons need variety and balance. As a rule of thumb, the younger children are, the more varied activities need to be.

For most children, there is no immediate need to learn English. Children also have different **learning preferences** and strengths. Younger children also tend to have limited concentration spans. For all these reasons, it is vital to provide variety and balance in lessons in order to maximise **engagement** and 'reach and teach' all the children in your classes effectively.

Some schools require you to complete lesson plan forms. There are also lesson plan templates online. Whatever you use, it is advisable to be consistent as this gives you an overall framework and provides a reusable record of what you have done.

In your lesson plan, you need variety and balance between time spent on **input,** instruction, activities and reflection. You also need to think about:

- Topics: varying the focus from topics close to the child's world to topics that are more exotic or link to other areas of the curriculum;
- Materials and resources: varying these to include authentic leaflets, picturebooks, websites or apps (see **78**);
- Activities and tasks: varying the types, focus, length, degree of challenge, and impact on children (see also **8** and **9**);
- Groupings: varying the way children work together, for example, in random, friendship, ability or mixed ability groupings;
- Skills: varying how you integrate language, social and thinking skills;
- Interaction patterns: varying who's talking to who and when, and making sure you optimise opportunities for children to interact;
- Movement: including opportunities for children to get up and move;
- Pace and mood: including short, quick-fire games as well as longer activities that require extended concentration;
- Choice: including elements of choice, such as when children choose who to work with or activities they'd like to do (see also **37**).

16 Plan in learning cycles

> By planning lessons in successive learning cycles you
> systematically build on children's learning and develop
> their metacognitive skills.

Learning cycles conceive learning as a cyclical rather than a linear
process. There are different models which you can adapt for language
teaching. Three useful ones are Plan, Do, Review, the 5E Learning Cycle
(Engage, Explore, Explain, Extend, Evaluate), particularly relevant for
CLIL or content-based lessons (see L), and an Accelerated Learning Cycle.

The Accelerated Learning Cycle has four main stages:

Stage 1 Connect: At the start of the lesson, you connect personally with
children to create a positive **affective climate** for learning. You link
previous learning to what children are going to learn and share learning
outcomes (see **14**). You also do activities to arouse children's interest,
find out what they already know and provide initial **input**.

Stage 2 Activate: Children do a sequence of **multi-sensory activities**
which support them in using language in ways that are meaningful
and purposeful. Children work in a variety of groupings and you
demonstrate and **model** language and thinking processes carefully.

Stage 3 Demonstrate: This stage provides varied opportunities for
children to demonstrate their learning, for example, by reporting back,
doing a role play, or giving a short presentation in plenary. Having
multiple opportunities to rehearse language (see **82**) and 'show they
know' boosts children's **self-esteem** and makes learning memorable.

Stage 4 Consolidate: Children review and reflect on what they have
learned and how (see **19**). This links back to the learning outcomes
shared in stage 1 and may include getting children to complete **self-
assessment** sheets or learning diaries (see **99**).

Smith, A., Lovatt, D. and Wise, D. (2004). *Accelerated Learning: A User's Guide*. Network
Continuum Education.

E: Learning how to learn

Learning how to learn is a process that takes place over time. Children progressively develop self-awareness and willingness to take responsibility for their own learning. They also gradually become able to manage, **monitor** and evaluate their progress and performance and develop independence and **autonomy**.

Learning how to learn involves developing children's **metacognitive** skills and **learning strategies**. This includes understanding *what* they are learning (the *product*), *why* they are learning it (the *purpose*), *how* they are learning (the *process*) and what they need to do to learn more (the *plan*). Children also need support and guidance in reflecting on their learning, identifying strategies that help them learn, assessing their achievement, and formulating what they can do to improve. Your role in this process as a **mediator**, motivator, model, and in creating a supportive and positive **affective climate** for learning, where children feel they can talk openly about their learning in either English, their mother tongue or **shared language**, is crucial (see also **100**).

My experience of introducing learning how to learn over many years suggests that it can take time, particularly for younger children, to fully appreciate the process. However, I've also found that once you integrate learning how to learn regularly in your lessons, children soon develop greater self-awareness, better work habits, increased confidence and a more active commitment to learning.

My key tips for learning how to learn are:

17 Integrate the development of learning strategies

18 Encourage active reflection on learning

19 Conduct regular learning reviews

20 Involve and inform parents

17 Integrate the development of learning strategies

> By integrating the development of learning strategies into lessons, you open children's eyes to techniques to help them learn. However, it's down to children's individual learning preferences whether or not they adopt them.

A **learning strategy** can be implemented either consciously or unconsciously. The more aware children are of learning strategies, the more likely they are to approach their learning in an effective and responsible way.

Learning strategies include **metacognitive**, cognitive and socio-affective strategies. Examples include encouraging children to:

- co-construct **success criteria** (see **14**);
- plan and reflect on learning, e.g. by using a KWLH grid (see **52**);
- memorise vocabulary and spell words correctly, e.g. by following the procedure 'look, say, cover, write, check' (see **55**);
- keep a conversation going by using the technique of adding information when you respond to a question, e.g. *Do you like ice cream? Yes, I do. Strawberry ice cream is my favourite*;
- communicate meaning when you don't know a word, e.g. by using mime and/or saying *It's a thing to …* (e.g. *open the door*);
- carry out cognitive tasks such as finding the differences between two pictures, for example, by systematically comparing each object in the pictures from left to right and top to bottom in turn.

Learning strategies are best taught as part of everyday classroom activities. You need to explain the purpose and **model** the strategy clearly. With younger children, it may be suitable to use a **think aloud** procedure with a puppet for this. You also need to provide varied opportunities for children to practise using the learning strategy in context.

Once you have introduced a learning strategy, it helps to remind children whenever it might be suitable to use again. It's also beneficial to encourage children to evaluate how helpful they find the strategy as part of a **learning review** (see **19**), and to listen to and respect their views.

Encourage active reflection on learning

> **Active reflection on learning develops children's self-knowledge and the ability to talk about themselves as people and as learners. It is often possible to adapt familiar classroom activities to achieve this.**

In order to encourage active reflection on learning, you need to create a caring classroom in which you listen to children and show that you value and respect their individual differences, preferences and contributions. You also need to use questions effectively (see **49**) and give children adequate time to reflect on their learning, for example, when establishing learning **outcomes**, negotiating **success criteria** (see **14**), conducting **learning reviews** (see **19**), **peer** and **self-assessment**, and **assessment for learning** (see **99** and **100**).

Other procedures and activities include:

- Keep a portfolio or progress journal: children develop a paper or online **portfolio** or progress journal in which they record personal information about their school, family and languages, and build up an individualised record of their work (see also **98**).
- Draw a picture: children draw pictures to illustrate an aspect of their learning, for example, *How I like learning English*. They then take turns to talk about their pictures (see also **99**).
- Order statements: children order statements, for example, in relation to the usefulness of vocabulary **learning strategies**, such as: *I repeat the word. / I write the translation. / I draw a picture. / I test myself.* They then compare and talk about their order.
- True or false: children identify personally true and false statements, for example, from a list of reasons for learning English, such as: *It will help me pass exams. / It's interesting and I enjoy it. / My parents want me to.* They then compare and talk about their views.
- Play a game: children play games adapted to promote reflection on learning. For example, use Sentence tennis (see also **25**) to get children to identify their learning strengths: *I'm good at remembering words. / I'm good at spelling* or to talk about their progress after a unit of work: *I can name wild animals. / I can tell the story.*

19   Conduct regular learning reviews

> By conducting regular learning reviews, children learn to monitor and evaluate their progress. This gives them greater responsibility and ownership of their learning.

A suggested procedure for carrying out a **learning review** at the end of a lesson is as follows:

1. Refer back to the learning **outcomes** and **success criteria** (see **14**) established at the start of the lesson.
2. Ask, e.g. *What did we do ... (first / next / then)? Why did we ...?* Children **recall** the sequence of lesson activities and identify the purpose of each one. Be ready to use prompts and reminders as necessary.
3. Ask further questions about each activity, e.g. *What did you learn when we played the game / acted out the story?* Encourage personal, divergent responses and make it clear there are no right answers.
4. Extend children's thinking by asking, e.g. *How did the ... help you learn? / What strategies did you use to ...?*
5. Ask children for personal views, e.g. *Did you like the ...? Why / Why not?* Listen to their responses.
6. With reference to the learning outcomes and success criteria, ask, e.g. *How well did you do?* If you like, children use a three-point scale of thumbs up, down or horizontal to respond.
7. Ask, e.g. *What do you plan to do to remember today's lesson?* and listen to the children's responses, e.g. *play the game with my mum.*

Learning reviews can be carried out either in the children's **shared language** or in English or, possibly, in a well-balanced mixture whereby English is used to talk about familiar activity types and the learning content, and the shared language is used to express more complex ideas about the learning process.

Once children are familiar with reviewing their learning, you can vary the procedure, for example, by getting children to conduct peer reviews or using activities such as those suggested in **18** (see also **99** and **100**).

Involve and inform parents

Parents have a profound influence on children's learning and it's crucial to involve them. You also need to be willing to listen and respond to their concerns sensitively.

Parents are usually keen to support their children's education. However, they may have had a very different experience of learning English and lack confidence in their linguistic ability to support their children. They may also have unrealistic expectations about the level of English their child can achieve by starting so young.

Examples of how to involve parents in their children's learning include:

- Communicate course information: regularly provide information about the aims, topics, materials and methodology you are using.
- Provide guidelines to support learning: suggest ideas to support children's learning at home, for example, encouraging children to teach their family songs and games they learn in class.
- Set realistic expectations: take time to ensure that parents' expectations of learning are realistic. Underline that potential benefits are not just linguistic but social, cognitive, psychological, emotional and cultural as well.
- Take learning home: for example, if children are keeping a **portfolio** or progress journal (see **18**), encourage them to regularly share and talk about this with their parents.
- Invite parents to watch a recording of a lesson: video one of your lessons (with parental permission and assurance that it will not be shown publicly). Use this as an opportunity to enhance parents' understanding of the way their children are learning English.
- Be available: in addition to regular progress meetings, make it clear that you're willing to talk to parents if they have concerns or queries. Remember that, although you're the expert on teaching, they're the expert on their child. Be open, honest, supportive and firm, if necessary, but also ready to learn from what parents have to say.

F: Storytelling

Stories provide shared contexts for natural language development and are a powerful vehicle for learning. Stories appeal to children's emotions and develop their imaginations. Stories also open children's minds to new ideas and engage them as thinkers with issues that are relevant and real.

I've had some memorable experiences using stories. Once, when visiting a country recently emerged from war, I was asked to demonstrate a storytelling lesson with 30 children, aged 9–12. I had never met the children before and did not speak their language. The story I chose was *Something Else*, a picturebook about **diversity** and **exclusion**. The children's response to the story, and the way they related it to their country's experience of war, was extraordinary. Their attempts to use every bit of English they had available to try to communicate to me, as an outsider to their country, their views about how wrong it is for people to exclude, hate and fight each other, were impressive. As well as bringing home to me the power of stories in a way I'll never forget, this experience led me to reflect how often we underestimate the maturity of children's thinking and how refreshingly open they can be in discussing complex issues that adults often shy away from.

My key tips for storytelling are:

21 **Select suitable stories**

22 **Make the most of the storytelling process**

23 **Exploit stories for learning (but don't spoil the pleasure!)**

24 **Go beyond stories**

Cave, K. and Riddell, C. (1994). *Something Else*. London: Puffin Books.

> The key to selecting suitable stories is to have clear
> criteria. You also need to be wary of texts and dialogues
> masquerading as stories but which, in reality, offer little
> more than structured language practice for its own sake.

There are many different sources for stories. These range from fairy
tales, and modern versions of fairy tales, to well-known, traditional
children's stories from the English-speaking world and other cultures.
They also include oral stories, picturebooks, graded readers, stories
from coursebooks, and digital and animated stories online.

Whatever the source of a story and its role in the teaching–learning process,
the most important criteria are age-appropriacy, interest and appeal to
children, and suitability of language. Other criteria to consider include:

- Story structure: is it a real story with a problem, conflict and
  resolution? Or is it a vehicle for language practice? The children
  won't be fooled!
- Narrative pattern: is there an identifiable narrative pattern that supports
  learning, e.g. repetitive, **cumulative,** question and answer, rhyme?
- Images: are they clear and attractive? Do they support
  understanding? (See also **91**.)
- Skills: what language, thinking and social skills can be developed
  through the story?
- Content: does this link to other areas of the curriculum?
- Culture: is cultural awareness and understanding enhanced?
- **Values**: what values are conveyed through the story? (See **31**.)
- **Global issues**: are issues such as social justice, climate change,
  diversity and gender equality addressed? (See **59**.)

Finally, you need to ask yourself what is the overall learning potential
and relevance of the story for children in terms of all of the above.

22 Make the most of the storytelling process

> By giving importance to the process of storytelling, you enhance the children's experience and achieve better outcomes.

The most usual way to use a story is as part of a series of lessons. Some key ideas to help you are:

- Plan in **learning cycles**: plan for children to return to the story two to four times over a series of lessons. Between each storytelling, children do related activities which progressively develop their ability to understand and use the story language (see also **16**).
- Tell the story yourself, at least initially: this enables you to support children's understanding and participation in real time. Use eye contact, facial expression, mime, gesture and your voice, including volume, speed, intonation and contrasting voices for different characters, to sustain **engagement**. Point to pictures, ask questions, pause, prompt, **elicit**, repeat or **recast** language, and encourage children to join in telling the story and/or doing actions as appropriate. Personalise the story by asking children if they like it and by getting them to relate it to their own experience.
- **Scaffold** children's responses: accept that initial responses may be partially in the children's mother tongue or **shared language**. Use techniques as above to increase responses and participation in English.
- Respect **diversity** and differentiation: the storytelling process allows everyone to participate successfully. Vary the way you invite children to participate, for example, **differentiate** the questions you ask (see **49**).
- Re-tell the story in different ways: each time you return to the story, avoid re-telling it in the same way as this is likely to feel repetitive. Vary what you do, for example, by getting children to hold up picture cards, move finger puppets or call out missing words. Alternatively, for some subsequent re-tellings, you may wish to use audio, video or digital versions of the story, if these are available.

Exploit stories for learning (but don't spoil the pleasure!)

> Stories lend themselves to a wide range of activities to develop language and skills. However, be careful not to allow narrowly focused language activities to dominate.

In addition to planning how to tell and re-tell a story, you need to prepare pre- and post-story activities which will support children's understanding and lead to desired learning **outcomes**.

Pre-story activities aim to capture children's curiosity and attention. They also provide an opportunity to pre-teach vocabulary. Examples of pre-story activities are:

- Say the title. Children predict the story. Use their predictions to motivate them and introduce relevant language.
- Show a scene from the story. Children describe the scene and hypothesise what happens before and/or afterwards.
- Show a character from the story. Children describe the character, predict if they are, e.g. good, bad, friendly, and their role in the story.
- Write four to six key words from the story on the board. Children predict how the words connect in the story.
- Show the front cover and read the blurb on the back of a picturebook and **elicit** children's response to introduce the story (see also **88**).

Post-story activities lead children from a global understanding to using more language. With older children, post-story activities may also include a focus on language awareness. Examples of post-story activities are:

- Order the story. Children sequence pictures or sentences.
- Act out the story.
- Re-tell the story using picture or word prompts.
- Write a story review, e.g. *I like … / My favourite character is …*.
- Play games based on the story, e.g. see **49** Roll a question.
- Identify language in the story, e.g. children circle past tense verbs.
- Do activities that go beyond the story (see **24**).

24 Go beyond stories

> When you do activities that go beyond stories, you take learning further and make it memorable. However, you also need to provide language support and show sensitivity in relating stories to children's own lives.

In many classrooms, exploitation of a story ends once children are familiar with its language. This misses the opportunity for deeper, more meaningful learning. There are a number of ways to achieve this:

- Thinking from within the story: children explore important issues through thinking about the characters' feelings and actions. You need to use guided questioning and be ready to extend and **recast** children's ideas. You also need to provide them with **functional language** to do more challenging activities using **higher-order thinking skills**. One example is a role play in which children resolve an issue in the story. Children prepare the role play based on role cards which provide language guidance and information about their character's point of view. Children then interact to resolve the problem creatively and express their ideas and opinions freely, including **translanguaging** (see also 44).
- Relating the story to children's own experience and lives: stories allow children to explore difficult issues, such as **exclusion,** in a safe way through talking about fictional characters rather than themselves. This needs to be handled sensitively and indirectly. For example, in a story about a character who is excluded at school, you might do an activity in which children think of five ways they can help a new child at their school. Relating stories to children's lives in this way also frequently links to **values** education (see **H**).
- Linking the story to **content-based learning**: if you're using a story such as Little Red Riding Hood, you might extend the story-related work to include content-based learning about forests or wolves.
- Linking the story to **intercultural competence** and **global issues**: this might involve getting children to compare cultural aspects of the story with their own (see also 43).

G: Playing games

Games provide a wide-ranging, flexible resource for developing children's language. Games promote natural communication and interaction and provide variety in mood, pace, skills, interaction patterns and physical movement. The same game can also often be played using different language and vocabulary with different ages and levels.

Many activities in primary have a game-like quality, for example, when you gradually reveal flashcards and children guess the words. However, games are different from other activities. Games have rules that need to be followed for the game to work fairly and successfully, and children are often more willing to follow the rules of games than they are other rules. Games also have goals, which give a purpose for using language and take the focus away from practising language for its own sake. Games also involve some kind of contest and may be competitive or cooperative. Winning a game, or attaining the goal of a game, may be the result of skill or chance or, most likely, a combination of both. Above all, games are fun.

I've had some of my best teaching moments when playing games with primary children. There's nothing more satisfying than being on the sidelines in a class full of children engrossed in autonomously playing a game using language you've taught them. On the other hand, games can also be divisive and lead to over-excitement and even aggression, if you don't set them up and manage them with care.

My key tips for playing games are:

25   **Competitive or cooperative?**

26   **Have games up your sleeve!**

27   **Use games to practise all skills.**

28   **Minimise the management risks**

25 Competitive or cooperative?

> Competitive and cooperative games have different benefits and drawbacks. However, it is often possible to set up games in a way that make the most of both.

Competitive games involve a contest between players. There is a winner and one or more losers. Examples of competitive games include board games and memory games. Competitive games generate enthusiasm and are motivating for many children. They reflect how real life works and provide opportunities for success. They also help children learn that 'a game is only a game' and to accept the outcome calmly. At the same time, some children always seem to either win or lose at competitive games. This can be demoralising, particularly for younger children.

Cooperative games involve a contest between players and a goal. An example of a cooperative game is Guess my word where children work in a group to ask *Yes/No* questions to deduce the word that only one child knows. Cooperative games develop children's willingness and ability to work together. However, they may unintentionally promote communication in the **shared language** and some children may opt out of making an effort to participate.

You can often make adjustments and keep the benefits of both types of games. In Word tennis, for example, children take turns to say words from a lexical set, e.g. food. The first child not to say a word loses the game. In an adjusted version, if a child can't think of a word they say 'Help!' If their partner can supply a word, the rally continues. At the end, the pair in the class with the longest rally are the winners. Similarly, in Kim's game, where children have one minute to memorise a set of real objects, flashcards, word cards or items in a poster, you can adjust the game so that children work in groups and note down what they can collectively remember (see also 58). The group who remembers most are the winners.

The combined benefits of competitive and cooperative games are also evident in activities, such as quizzes, where children work cooperatively within their teams but are motivated by the competitive element as well.

> It's useful to have a repertoire of games to play spontaneously. Games that need no preparation, no materials, and can be adapted for use with different ages and levels work best.

There are moments when it helps to play a game. These include when you need to liven up the mood, when children need to review language, or when you still have five minutes before the end of a lesson.

Two of my favourite games which can be used in this way are:

1   Spelling gym: Ask children to stand up and teach them actions for the game. Place your hands on your shoulders to start the game. For vowels, cross over your hands (i.e. right hand on left shoulder, left hand on right shoulder). For letters with a stem above the line, e.g. *d*: put your arms in the air. For letters with a stem below the line, e.g. *y*: put your arms down by your side. Spell familiar words. Say the letters, children do the actions and identify the words. Go faster as children become familiar with the game. Invite pairs of children to take turns to lead the game instead of you.

2   The grid game: Divide the class into two teams, e.g. circles and squares. Draw a grid of letters (3 × 3) on the board. Choose relevant letters such as initial letters of familiar vocabulary, e.g. I (for ice cream), answers to content-based questions, e.g. P (for *protein*), or language-based questions, e.g. W (*went*). The first team chooses a letter and you give a clue to guess the word, e.g. *The name of a food you eat in summer.* If the team answers correctly, you mark the letter with a circle or square. The first team to get three letters in a row are the winners. Children can also prepare their own grids and clues to play with the class.

It's also useful to have games up your sleeve for children to play independently if they finish work before the rest of the class. These can include board games, possibly ones which children have made themselves (see **40**), and/or sets of picture or word cards for games such as Pelmanism or Snap!

27 Use games to practise all skills

> Games develop listening, speaking, reading and writing
> skills as well as general learning, thinking and social skills.
> Games work most effectively when you focus on all the
> skills they develop, not just language.

In a board game where children use a dice and counters and ask and
answer questions such as *Can you count to a hundred in tens?* in pairs or
groups, they also need to follow rules, take turns, listen to each other (to
decide if the answer merits moving on a square), use classroom language,
such as *It's my turn!*, play fairly, and accept winning or losing with good
grace. In order to maximise learning **outcomes**, you need to explain and
model what's involved and show that you value children's efforts to play
cooperatively as much as their ability to answer the questions.

In a content-based, team reading game, you might hold up or project
one at a time true/false statements about the topic children are learning
about, e.g. mammals and reptiles. Children read the statements silently,
discuss with a partner, take turns to say whether the statements are true
or false, justify their answer and score points for their team. The game
not only develops silent reading skills in a light and enjoyable way, but
also develops children's ability to work together, categorise animals, give
reasons and justify their views.

In a group writing game on the same topic, such as Animal
consequences, you might project or write a list of six to eight categories
on the board, e.g. *size, colour, skin*. Children individually invent the
name of an animal and write it at the top of a strip of paper. They
then fold the paper over and pass it to the next child in the group who
writes a sentence about the size, e.g. *It's very big*, and so on. At the end,
children unfold their papers, read the descriptions, decide whether each
invented animal is a mammal or reptile, and choose (and possibly draw)
the one they like best. In this game, children individually contribute
sentences to a creative, collaborative outcome and use previously learnt
criteria to categorise their imaginary animals.

Minimise the management risks

> Games can be risky in terms of containing children's enthusiasm and controlling noise. The key to success lies in setting them up and managing them effectively.

The following is a checklist of what to do:

- Prepare language to explain the game before going into class, especially if you are playing it for the first time.
- Announce the name and purpose of the game, e.g. *We're going to play a game called … in order to …* . By teaching the names of games, you reduce the need for detailed instructions next time. By explaining the purpose, you explicitly link the game to children's learning (i.e. it's more than just fun).
- Rehearse and practise language for the game, including interactive language, such as *That's right / wrong. It's my / your turn!*
- Divide the class into pairs, groups or teams, as necessary.
- Keep instructions clear and divide them into stages (see **6**). Use gesture, mime or visuals to clarify meaning. Where possible, build in using English to the rules of the game, e.g. if children call out an answer in their **shared language**, they don't score a point.
- Demonstrate the game. In the case of a pair work game, this may mean playing the game with a child at the front of the class or playing the game with the whole class first.
- Check children understand what to do before starting the game. If necessary, ask a confident child to recap the rules in their shared language. This gives children an opportunity to hear the instructions repeated.
- Allow children to play the game independently and make it clear that you expect them to do this responsibly. Insist on the use of 'our quiet voices' (see **73**) if everyone is playing the game at the same time.
- **Monitor** discreetly and be fair and firm in reinforcing the rules.
- Stop the game before children lose interest.
- Actively look for positive things to say about the way individual children or the whole class has played the game.
- Conduct a **learning review** in order to encourage children to identify what and how the game has helped them to learn (see **19**).

Minimise the management risks | 35

H: Values education

Values are core attitudes and beliefs that underlie and influence the way we think and act in different situations. Values education is to do with guiding children's thinking and behaviour in order to help them to realise their individual potential and become responsible members of the community.

Values education refers to three main spheres of children's lives. These are:

1. the values that children hold in relation to themselves, such as honesty, reliability, perseverance and resilience;
2. the values that children hold in relation to others, such as kindness, empathy, tolerance and respect;
3. the values that children hold towards the world around them, such as looking after the environment, the treatment of animals and issues of social justice.

Although parents are the main influence in the formation of children's values, teachers have a significant role to play. My experience over the years has convinced me that, through systematically integrating values education into everything you do in the classroom, you not only foster children's sense of wellbeing (see 57) and develop positive relationships (see 5) but are also more likely to achieve better academic and language learning **outcomes** as well. However, it's also important to remember that values education is a complex, dynamic process, rather than a checklist of items to be learnt. It takes place gradually over time in harmony with other aspects of children's **cognitive**, emotional, social and psychological **development**.

My key tips for values education are:

29 **Be aware of your role**

30 **Focus on values close to the child's world**

31 **Use a tool kit of values activities**

32 **Promote effort and resilience**

Children learn values in different ways over time. Your role in this is crucial.

Everything you do in the classroom, from the way you greet children to the way you manage learning, praise children or tell them off, gives a message about your own **values**. Here are four key ways to integrate positive values into your everyday teaching:

- Socialisation: children learn values when their habits are approved or not by the adults around them, and they understand the reasons for this. If you insist on, and acknowledge, the use of 'please' and 'thank you' in order to be polite, children internalise this behaviour and learn to recognise its value. If you explain why you don't approve a particular behaviour, e.g. *Sit down, please, Rachida – Ahmed can't see the story*, you encourage the value of learning to think about others, and not only yourself.
- Being a role model: be aware of your own language and behaviour and 'walk the talk'. You can only expect to influence children positively if you also display the values you wish to promote. Many values are a two-way street: if you wish children to show you and their peers respect, then you need to show them respect too; if you wish children to listen to you and each other, then you need to listen to them too. If you get angry and shout at children, then don't be surprised if they also show anger and raise their voices too.
- Encouraging thinking about values: use appropriate opportunities to encourage children to notice and express opinions about values in relation to themselves and their world. These may come from stories or other texts or be prompted by something else, e.g. the arrival of a new child in the class, or getting to know each other's languages (see also **44**).
- Teaching the language of values: introduce and use vocabulary related to relevant values, such as *kind, helpful*. This makes children explicitly aware of the concepts and encourages them to express their views and think about their own actions.

30 Focus on values close to the child's world

> Values need to be part of a context that children can relate to and understand. This makes values meaningful and encourages children to think and act responsibly.

It's best to focus on here-and-now **values** in the children's immediate environment before focusing on values at school, home and in the wider community. One example is a willingness to take turns when speaking, to listen to what others have to say without interrupting, and to show respect for views that may be different from your own. One way to do this is through Circle time.

In Circle time, children sit or stand in a circle and take turns to express their views by completing a sentence, e.g. *I think the story is … because … / The most worrying thing about global warming is … .* The rules are that you only speak when it's your turn, you say *Pass* if you don't wish to speak, and you use the **shared language** if you need to. With lower primary, children pass an object, such as a toy microphone, round the circle as a visual signal of whose turn it is to speak. With upper primary, two children can build up a mind map on the board as others speak. At the end, this can be reviewed and lead into e.g. writing about global warming. When done regularly, children soon realise that Circle time gives everyone an equal opportunity to speak and be listened to. This makes it easier to establish the value of respectful listening and turn-taking in other areas of classroom interaction too.

Another example of a value within children's immediate context is when you teach multilingual classes and wish to communicate the value of equal respect for all their languages (see also **44**). One activity is, over time, to get children to take turns to teach a short dialogue in (one of) their home language(s) to you and the class. As well as being enjoyable and giving exposure to different languages, children gain a sense of **self-esteem** and pride from interest in their languages and teaching these to others. This activity also leads to discussion of similarities and differences between languages and the value of learning languages in today's global world.

Children benefit from varied opportunities to expand their understanding of values. Activities that you use in your everyday teaching are often suitable for this.

Many classroom materials and activities can be adapted to focus on **values** education. Examples include:

1. Picturebooks and stories: these often reflect significant issues such as loneliness, bullying or **exclusion**. The focus on fictional characters raises awareness of values in a non-threatening way and, with appropriate questioning, e.g. *How does ... feel? What would you do?*, encourages children to reflect and apply positive values to themselves (see also **24**).
2. Drama and roleplay: this includes improvisation or role plays, with previously prepared role cards, based on values-based situations, such as cheating in an exam or stealing a bar of chocolate. Roleplay and drama gets children to think and act out how they might respond.
3. Games and activities with a values focus: one example is a values' clarification activity based on the UN Rights of the Child. Children individually identify three rights that they think are most important. They then get together, first in pairs and then groups, to justify and finalise their choices before comparing these with the whole class.
4. Songs, poems, rhymes and raps: there are many that touch on values themes relating to self, others or the environment. However, you also need to plan follow-up activities that focus on discussion and application of these values in order to ensure that the themes are not dealt with in a simplistic way.
5. Reflection and discussion: encourage children to express their views on values-related issues, for example, by preparing agree / disagree statements on the topic and teaching **functional language** and **chunks**, e.g. *In my view ...*, which children can use to express and justify their views. You can prepare simple **substitution tables** to support children's speaking, e.g. *I agree / disagree because ... .*

UN Convention on the Rights of the Child in Child Friendly Language (1989).

32 Promote effort and resilience

> By promoting the values of effort and resilience, you develop children's capacity to persevere in the face of learning challenges. This increases their self-esteem.

Effort is to do with trying hard to achieve a goal and resilience is the ability to continue trying despite difficulties and mistakes. Both qualities underpin children's self-belief that they can achieve if they try.

Carol Dweck's research identifies two responses to setbacks among children with equal skills: those who give up and those who persevere. The difference is attributed to children's beliefs about why they failed. Children with a 'fixed mindset' believe that their intelligence is something they are born with and unchangeable. They feel their mistakes are due to a lack of ability and there's no point trying. They also avoid challenges since these are likely to lead to more mistakes. By contrast, children with a 'growth mindset' believe that their intelligence can be developed through effort and hard work. They feel their mistakes are due to a lack of effort and can be remedied by hard work. These children embrace challenges as opportunities to learn. They feel resilient in the face of setbacks and motivated to improve.

In order to develop a 'growth mindset' in children you need to:

- Create an atmosphere in which the children feel valued (see **70**).
- Convey the attitude that mistakes are opportunities for learning.
- Make sure the level of challenge is appropriate.
- Use descriptive praise that focuses on the process of what children achieve, particularly commending their effort and persistence (see **11**).
- Focus on children's strengths and what they can do.
- Provide materials or technology that motivate children to make an effort, for example, creating a digital quiz (see also **89**).
- Talk about effort and resilience in relation to other activities, for example, if you use traditional stories such as The ant and grasshopper.

Dweck, C. (2007). *Mindset: The New Psychology of Success.* New York: Ballantine Books.

I: Songs, rhymes, chants and raps

Songs, rhymes, chants and raps are frequently used in most primary classrooms – and for good reasons. They develop listening and speaking skills and provide opportunities for movement and drama. They are also memorable and provide enjoyable repetition practice which reinforces pronunciation, vocabulary, language **chunks** and grammatical structures in a contextualised way.

When every child is engaged at the same time in singing a song or saying a rhyme, chant or rap, this creates a sense of community and class identity. It also allows shy children to participate without risking exposure, which boosts their confidence and **self-esteem**. Songs, rhymes, chants and raps also encourage children to take English home as, for example, when they spontaneously repeat what they have learnt to parents and siblings.

However, in order to achieve positive results with songs, rhymes, chants and raps, you need to choose them carefully and exploit them in ways that enhance and extend children's enjoyment and learning. Evidence of this may come, for example, when children take ownership of a song, rhyme, rap or chant and use it independently. One example from my own teaching is a group of lower primary children who, after learning the traditional rhyme and game, Queenie, queenie, who's got the ball? in class, were later spotted playing it independently in the playground. Another example is a group of upper primary children who chose to learn by heart the long, and quite complex, lyrics of a current pop song in order to make a karaoke dance video as part of a project.

My key tips for songs, rhymes, chants and raps are:

33   Make the most of music (not just songs!)

34   Use songs, rhymes, chants and raps for different purposes

35   Vary your teaching techniques

36   Invent your own songs, raps and chants!

33 Make the most of music (not just songs!)

> Music in primary language classrooms is usually associated with songs. However, music by itself is also an invaluable resource to support children's learning.

It's helpful to have music available for different occasions and activities. This includes calm, relaxing classical music and lively, dance music, as well as karaoke versions of songs, that you and the children enjoy.

Music changes the mood. You can use music to liven children up or, perhaps more frequently, to calm them down. You can also use music to accompany routine activities, such as tidying up the classroom, and as background to help children concentrate on individual work. You can also use music for specific activities and games.

Examples of how to make the most of music include:

- Visualisations: use music to accompany short visualisations, for example, when setting the scene before telling a story.
- Musical associations: play short extracts of different kinds of music. Children listen and associate the music with, for example, a feeling, a colour or an animal. They then compare their responses.
- Musical pictures: play an extract of music. Children draw a picture that reflects the music. They then describe their pictures.
- Music to inspire a story: play an extract of music, for example, a dramatic moment in a film, such as a car chase. Children work in pairs to imagine what is happening and who is involved. They then use this as the basis for creating a story.
- Musical games: use music to play games, for example, Musical bumps. Play music and children dance. Pause the music and say, e.g. *Everyone who's wearing something red!* These children sit on the floor as fast as they can and the last one loses a point (out of three).
- Musical time limits: use music to time an activity. Children have until the music stops to complete the activity.

Use songs, rhymes, chants and raps for different purposes

> Songs, rhymes, chants and raps can be used for many different purposes. You need to select them carefully and ensure they are suitable for the age group.

When selecting a song, rhyme, chant, you need to consider the purpose(s) for using it. You also need to examine the balance of new and familiar language and the relevance to the syllabus and topic, story or unit of work children are currently doing. It's also important to consider the clarity and speed of the recording (if you're using one), and the appeal and memorability of the rhythm or tune. Above all, you need to make sure that the song, rhyme, chant or rap you select is **age-appropriate**. There's nothing more likely to produce a negative response from children than if they feel that a song, rhyme, rap or chant is babyish. It also helps if you feel enthusiastic about teaching it too.

In many cases, your choice of song, rhyme, rap or chant will fulfil more than one purpose. Some purposes, illustrated with traditional examples, are:

- Developing listening skills: longer songs and rhymes with a wider range of language and vocabulary are likely to be suitable, for example, songs or rhymes that tell a story such as There was a princess long ago or The bear hunt. With upper primary, some pop songs or raps may also be appropriate.
- Recycling vocabulary: songs with repetition of vocabulary from the same lexical set, for example, One finger, one thumb, keep moving.
- Consolidating grammar: songs with repetition of the language structure you want children to practise, for example, The Music Man.
- Extending work on a story: songs that relate to the story, such as When Goldilocks went to the house of the bears.
- Extending work on a topic: songs that relate to the topic, for example, Little Peter Rabbit, if children are learning about pets.
- Linking to **content-based learning**: songs that relate to the content, for example, I hear thunder, if children are learning about seasons and weather.

35 Vary your teaching techniques

> There are many techniques for teaching songs, rhymes, chants and raps. By varying these, you keep children engaged and get them to participate in increasingly independent and creative ways.

Although it's possible to teach songs, rhymes, chants and raps by getting children to repeat each line in turn, this is likely to be boring and make them lose interest. It's much more effective to adopt a global approach in which you systematically lead children from understanding the whole song, rhyme, rap or chant, to becoming familiar with its rhythm or tune and joining in saying or singing it themselves.

Examples of guided and freer techniques include:

- Children point to flashcards on the classroom walls or hold up picture cards, when they hear key words.
- Children hold up finger or pencil puppets and join in when different characters are speaking or singing.
- Children do actions to accompany the song, rhyme, rap or chant.
- Children use percussion instruments to keep the rhythm.
- Conduct the class as an orchestra (they sing or speak loudly when you raise your hands and softly when you lower them).
- Children identify rhyming words or supply missing words.
- Vary the patterns of participation, for example, groups take turns to sing or say and act out one verse each.
- Children sing a song as a round. Group A sings the first line of the song. Group B starts as soon as Group A finishes.
- Use a karaoke version and children can also invent a dance.
- Children substitute vocabulary with other words of their choice.
- Children adapt or create their own versions.

Invent your own songs, raps and chants!

> Although there are many online and other sources for songs, raps and chants, you can't always find exactly what you're looking for. In this case, the best solution is to invent your own!

Songs, raps and chants may or may not rhyme. The basic differences are that songs have music with a tune and lyrics, raps and chants are spoken monologues or exchanges with informal language, repetition and a strong rhythm and beat. Raps are usually set to music.

To invent a song, think of the vocabulary and language you wish to include, for example, names, body parts and adjectives to describe wild animals. Think of a tune either from a traditional song in English or from the children's culture, or from a song they know and like. Create a song by combining the language and tune. Make sure that the lines scan correctly, including word and sentence stress. Practise singing the song you have invented and make any changes needed before going into class. An example based on the traditional tune of Here we go round the mulberry bush might be:

A tiger has got big, sharp claws / Big, sharp claws / Big, sharp claws / A tiger has got big, sharp claws / Make sure you keep away! with additional verses, e.g. *A crocodile's got enormous teeth.*

To invent a rap or chant, think of the vocabulary and language you wish to include, for example, after school activities, and related rhyming words e.g. *school / cool.* Familiarise yourself with recordings of raps and chants to get the idea of the rhythm, beat and pace. Create a rap or chant. Click your fingers, clap or use percussion to keep the rhythm and beat. Practise and adjust, as for songs above. An example might be:

What do you do every day after school? / On Monday, I go swimming – and it's cool. with additional verses for other days and activities, e.g. *Tuesday / play basketball.*

J: Working with projects

A project is individual or collaborative work done over time which leads to a final **outcome**. A project engages children in using their language, social and thinking skills and competences in a naturally integrated and holistic way. A project can also inspire children to explore beyond the limits of their current competences in ways that are meaningful.

Projects provide a personalised learning challenge and children feel motivated to produce high quality work. Projects promote communication and interaction and frequently incorporate other areas of the curriculum, such as science. Projects develop thinking skills, such as problem solving. They also encourage learner **autonomy,** and develop positive **values** and social skills, such as cooperation. Projects also give children an opportunity to build on other strengths they may have, for example, if they are artistic.

However, working with projects is not always easy. Noise levels may soar, some children may be **off task** and there may be unnecessary time-wasting, such as when children get distracted carrying out online research. It's sometimes difficult to **monitor** the language children are using. There's also a risk that children may copy online texts into their projects, thinking that you will not notice.

So, is it worth it? The answer is a resounding yes, but only if projects are set up carefully and managed effectively. In my experience, there's nothing more rewarding than children working together as a team to produce a project which they have chosen, planned and carried out by themselves, even though your support in the background is also crucial.

My key tips for working with projects are:

37 **Offer children choice**

38 **Remember the 4 Ms!**

39 **Integrate classroom language**

40 **Use projects as the basis of other activities**

By offering children choice, you empower and motivate them. It helps if the choices offered are clear and specific.

Choice gives children **agency** and develops their ability to take decisions and have control of their learning. Children develop **autonomy** and become more willing to take responsibility for their work. This leads to a sense of ownership and willingness to make an effort (see also **32**). It also helps make learning personalised and memorable.

When working with projects, you can offer children choice in different ways. This includes choice over the content and format of the project, and who children work with. It may be helpful to present choices using a choice board (see **52** and **72**).

For example, in relation to a project on wild animals, children might choose between producing, either on paper or digitally, i) a fact file on a wild animal of their choice; ii) a leaflet about wild animals in danger of extinction; iii) a book about wild animals in their country.

In relation to a project on food, where the content is to produce a report on healthy eating, children might choose between the following formats for presenting their projects: i) an electronic presentation; ii) a poster; iii) a video.

In a lower primary project where, for example, children create farm animals from templates in order to collaboratively produce a class display of a farm, children might choose, firstly, the animal they wish to make and, secondly, whether to decorate it with i) crayons; ii) finger paints; iii) small balls of tissue paper (and glue).

Although friendship groupings for projects work well, some children may feel excluded. For behaviour management reasons, it may also be better if you decide the children in each group. In order for children to accept this, it may help to play a game whereby you give each child a picture card and they identify other members of their group with the same cards. Although the outcome appears random, it allows you to still be in control of who works with who.

38 Remember the 4 Ms!

> The 4 Ms are: motivation, modelling, monitoring and
> mileage. Together they give you a flexible framework for
> managing projects effectively.

Projects may last a week or a school year. Some projects are collaborative
from the outset, such as making a video. Others involve individual
contributions to a collaborative outcome, such as creating an e-zine.

Whatever the project, you need to consider:

1   Motivation: make sure there's a reason and purpose for doing
    the project that children can relate to. If possible, show children
    an example of a completed project. This gives them a vision of
    the **outcome** and engages them emotionally. If you offer children
    choices (see **37**), ensure that these align with their interests and feel
    worthwhile.
2   Modelling: talk through the preparation, materials and procedures.
    Rehearse key language and **model** research and thinking skills. Go
    through stages of the project (a flow chart is often useful – see **52**)
    and establish or negotiate **success criteria** (see **14**).
3   Monitoring: make sure children follow the project plan and set time
    limits. **Monitor** and vary the support you give children according
    to their ability and needs. Be aware of what every group is doing –
    develop eyes in the back of your head, but don't breathe down their
    necks! Encourage children to work independently and use each other
    as a resource. Give constructive **feedback** and praise as appropriate
    (see **11** and **32**).
4   Mileage: this refers to the amount of use and learning children get
    out of their projects. Give children opportunities to present their
    projects and encourage peer feedback and questions. Conduct a
    learning review (see **19**) and get children to self-assess their projects
    (see **99**). Use projects as the basis of other activities (see **40**) and
    share them with parents to reinforce the home–school link (see **20**).

> Make children aware that interacting in English during project work is a valuable part of the learning process. At the same time, recognise that children's shared language also has a valuable role to play.

Children do not learn to use classroom language in English by magic.

You need to explain the importance of classroom language and provide natural opportunities to use English as the principal means of communication. You also need to create a classroom climate in which children are willing to take risks, use English as much as possible, and see mistakes as learning opportunities. As well as insisting (gently) on their using English whenever they can, you also need to respect that, at times, using their **shared language** is more effective and helpful.

Three examples of ways to integrate classroom language into project work are:

1 Teach project-related vocabulary: introduce words that relate to the project, for example, *research, report, poster, survey, chart.*
2 Classroom language signs: display language relevant to the project, e.g. *Let's look at the website. / I want to find out about X.*
3 Jumbled sentences: prepare sets of word cards to make sentences and questions of relevant classroom language. Before the project, children work in pairs, order the cards, and write the sentences in their notebooks for reference.

In addition to encouraging the use of classroom language, you need to **differentiate** between children's **on task** and **off task** use of their shared language. If children use this to plan, strategise or make decisions during project work, then this is legitimate and likely to lead to deeper learning and better **outcomes**, whereas a social chat about what to do in break time is not.

40 Use projects as the basis of other activities

Children's completed projects provide a varied resource of materials to enrich and extend learning. By using their projects for other activities, you show that you value children's work and boost their self-esteem.

When children become aware that their projects are likely to be used for other activities, this motivates them to produce their best quality work. Some examples of ways you can exploit children's projects are:

- Project quiz: this is suitable for posters, fact files, descriptions or reports. Children write two quiz questions based on their project. Divide the class into teams. The teams take turns to ask and answer the quiz questions. The team with most correct answers wins.
- Project exhibition: this is suitable for paper projects as above. Prepare questions or true/false statements based on the projects. Children circulate in pairs, read the projects and find the answers.
- Project riddles: this is suitable for arts and craft projects, e.g. paper plates of food made from modelling clay. Prepare riddles, e.g. *It's got a biscuit, an apple and a banana.* Say the riddles and children identify the projects. Children can also prepare the riddles themselves.
- Project read-alouds: this is suitable for projects where children make books (see **63**) with factual information or a story. Choose one of the children's project books to read to the class. Children can also read their books to each other.
- Project games: this is suitable for projects where children make board games. Children choose and play each other's games (see also **26**).
- Project vote: **elicit** and agree criteria for judging the projects. Children decide their favourite (excluding their own) and either vote in an online poll or write the name on a piece of paper. Use the results to identify the three best projects.

K: Intercultural competence

The aim of intercultural competence is to prepare children to become curious, open-minded citizens who can live their lives positively with cultural **diversity** as the norm.

Intercultural competence is made up of knowledge, skills, attitudes and awareness. Knowledge includes facts about a culture and knowing how to behave in a culturally appropriate way. Skills include the ability to interact with people respectfully, and to find out things about another culture. Attitudes include a willingness to see things from another point of view. Awareness includes having a sense of your own identity and being able to relate another culture to your own.

In lower primary your approach needs to focus on getting children to participate in pleasurable cultural activities such as songs and games that may be similar to ones they know in their home language(s). As children develop, intercultural competence includes comparing and contrasting aspects of culture from the English-speaking world with their own. It also extends to learning about diverse cultures in the wider world and opportunities to interact in an intercultural communicative context.

In my experience, the starting point for developing intercultural competence is often in children's own classrooms where pupils from different ethnic, cultural, social and language backgrounds work and play together.

My key tips for intercultural competence are:

41 Integrate culture appropriately

42 Compare and contrast cultures

43 Explore culture in the wider world

44 Value children's multilingual identities

41 Integrate culture appropriately

> Traditional children's culture offers a rich resource
> for learning and encourages pleasure in participation.
> However, as children get older, contemporary and pop
> culture is likely to be more appropriate.

In lower primary, the integration of traditional songs, rhymes, games and stories encourages children to join in activities that may be familiar from their home languages. Traditional counting songs, which exist in many languages, such as Five little ducks, are examples of this, where holding up fingers to count and acting out the songs, promotes **engagement** as well as gives exposure to meaningful language.

Traditional rhymes, such as Incy Wincy Spider, provide exposure to different sounds, rhythm and stress patterns, and contribute to children's pronunciation and literacy development. The same is true with traditional stories, such as Little Red Riding Hood, which may also be familiar in the mother tongue, and where children take pleasure in repetitive refrains, such as *What big eyes you've got!*

Children also often delight in learning traditional games, such as Paper, scissors, stone or Can I cross your river, Mr Crocodile?, and may be inspired to play them independently. When children learn traditional customs to celebrate festivals, such as trick or treating at Halloween, they may also teach them to parents and siblings at home.

As children get older, you need to integrate culture in a way that reflects their increased maturity, or they will feel patronised and demotivated. In upper primary, contemporary popular culture is likely to be more appropriate. Current pop songs that have suitable lyrics are a good option, especially if children choose these themselves. Modern versions of fairy tales are popular too and can also act as a springboard for discussion of **values** such as gender equality or greed (see also **31**).

Compare and contrast cultures

> By comparing and contrasting other cultures with their own, children develop an understanding of similarities and differences between themselves and others. This also helps them to build up a sense of their own identity.

Through learning about others, children learn about themselves. In finding out about other cultures and ways of behaviour, children reflect on their own local, regional or national culture and ways of doing things and build up a picture of their own cultural identity. This may be in relation to the language(s) they speak, festivals they celebrate or any other aspect of their lives and the society they live in.

In order to be meaningful, cultural comparisons and contrasts need to be grounded in children's immediate world. One activity is to prepare short descriptions of a typical day of children who live in an English-speaking culture, such as Britain, including details of daily routines such as what time they get up, when they start and finish school, what they have for lunch, and when they go to bed. Circulate the descriptions and learners read and note the information that is the same as or different from their own lives in two columns. This leads to a discussion of what learners find out that surprises them, for example, in my experience in Spain, the shorter school day of British children, having a packed lunch, and earlier bedtime. A follow-up activity might include getting children to write about their typical day with a view to explaining it to others, or to do a collaborative project on some aspect, such as planning a week's menu of their ideal school lunches.

Another cultural activity that primary children enjoy is comparing the kinds of jokes they find funny along the lines of: *What's the hottest day of the week? / Sunday* or *How do bees go to school? / On the school buzz.* In this case, there's the satisfaction of being able to understand and appreciate simple play on words and re-tell a joke in another language. This is motivating and also helps to promote a positive attitude and affinity with English.

43 Explore culture in the wider world

Learning about culture in the wider world expands children's horizons and introduces them to issues of social justice. However, you need to take care to avoid cultural stereotypes.

There are many ways of introducing children to culture in the wider world. A popular theme is to find out about food from around the world. In classes with children from diverse backgrounds, this can also be accompanied by organised tastings of foods (ask for permission and check children's allergies first). For example, children might bring to class Indian samosas or Polish poppy seed cake and be ready to answer questions about the ingredients and say when they eat the food in their culture. Children who try the food describe the taste and say whether they like it and have anything similar in their culture. With older children, the theme of global food can also be expanded to explore issues of social justice related to the UN Sustainable Development Goals, such as poverty and hunger.

One of the most effective ways of promoting **intercultural competence** is by using picturebooks. These use creative and insightful ways to open children's eyes to a wide range of different cultural perspectives, such as everyday life in rural Africa, and issues of social justice, such as being caught up in war and becoming a refugee. Traditional folk tales from around the world, such as the Anansi stories, originally from Ghana, or The blind men and the elephant from India can also provide fresh cultural perspectives on relevant and important issues, as well as raise children's awareness that all cultures have a wealth of well-known, traditional stories, not just their own (see also **24**).

When you introduce children to culture from the wider world, you need to be careful not to present stereotypical images and notions of other cultures that may create or reinforce prejudices. If you have children of different cultural backgrounds in your classes, one constructive way round this is to invite parents, who speak English, to give a short talk, or lead a Q and A session, on some aspect of their culture and get children to prepare questions to ask in advance. Alternatively, older children can lead these sessions themselves.

Value children's multilingual identities

> Languages children speak are a key factor in their identity and a significant resource for learning. By valuing children's multilingual identities, you promote intercultural competence, develop self-esteem and create a positive affective climate for learning.

These days it is not infrequent to have children in your classes who speak several languages. Rather than excluding children's languages from the English classroom, it is more constructive to build on their **multilingual identities** for learning and developing intercultural understanding. This creates an **inclusive** learning climate and a sense of pride and belonging. It can also lead to greater **engagement** as well as better performance.

Some examples of ways to promote children's multilingualism are:

1. Children draw pictures to show their different languages and the people they use them with. Use the pictures to get children to talk about their languages and to feel a sense of pride in them.

2. Make references to children's languages. For example, ask, *Does anyone know a word for this in another language?* Or, *Is this the same in your language?*

3. Let children teach you their languages. At appropriate moments, give children an opportunity to teach you and others something from one of their languages. Show your interest in this and let them enjoy correcting and praising you, just as you do them!

4. Allow **translanguaging** (see also **30**) when children are trying to express their ideas and opinions (see also **24**). Reconstruct and **recast** what children are saying, with the help of other children if necessary.

5. Consider getting children to use another language for writing. There are times when this can be beneficial, for example, when keeping a learning diary or writing a **learning review**.

L: Content-based learning (CLIL)

Content-based learning has been around for many years. In its most recent form, Content and Language Integrated Learning (CLIL) is an approach which explicitly reflects the connection between language and subject learning. School subjects, or parts of subjects, are taught through English with the aim of developing both at the same time. The subject determines the content-related vocabulary, language structures and functions that will be taught and children are given extensive language support in order to make learning possible.

However, CLIL varies in different contexts. In a strong or hard version, the principal focus is on the subject content and related academic skills, and so is content-driven. In a weak or soft version, the focus is more on language learning, and so is more language-driven. Primary ELT programmes, which include a strand of content-based learning, are sometimes described as soft or weak versions of CLIL. This is because the underlying rationale for including content is that it provides a context for practising language from a language syllabus. The extent of subject vocabulary and related academic language and skills taught in a soft version of CLIL may also be diluted.

Whatever your teaching situation, content-based learning helps to make learning English challenging and purposeful. It also develops children's academic and communicative skills in ways that are engaging and enjoyable.

My key tips for content-based learning are:

45   Choose and plan appropriate content

46   Vary the skills and practice activities

47   Support understanding of content and language

48   Adapt activities from other areas of the curriculum

> In order to choose and plan appropriate content, you need to have clear criteria. You also need to prepare activities that make a coherent learning sequence.

You may be choosing and planning content either to complement your coursebook, or to fit in with the school curriculum, or to develop a content-based unit of work in its own right. The time scale may be anything from a single lesson to half a term. Whatever the purpose and length of time, you need to above all consider age-appropriacy of the content and children's potential interest and motivation. You also need to identify thinking and language skills and consider the balance of cognitive and linguistic challenge. A further criterion is to what extent the content builds on children's current knowledge or introduces concepts that are new. It's also helpful to think about whether the content will provide opportunities for investigative enquiry and **cooperative learning**, leading to self-directed project work (see **J**) or other creative **outcomes**.

One way to explore whether or not the content is suitable is to complete a content map or grid. Write the name of the content area in the centre of the map or at the top of the grid, for example, *The water cycle* or *Food groups*. Around the map or in the first column of the grid, note possible activities. For each activity, extend the map or columns in the grid by noting:

- language and vocabulary (receptive, productive, familiar and new);
- skills and competences (language, thinking and social skills);
- attitudes and **values** (in relation to self, others, environment; see **H**);
- concepts (known and new);
- curriculum links (to other subjects such as science, music or maths).

Ideally, each activity in your map or grid should be like the link in a chain. In other words, each activity should both build on what comes before and prepare for what follows, thereby forming an integrated learning sequence or cycle (see **16**). If you work in a soft CLIL context and notice that there is a lot of new language as well as new concepts in your completed map or grid, you may feel that the content is too challenging and want to make changes.

46   **Vary the skills and practice activities**

> As with other lessons, you need to vary the skills and practice
> activities in content-based learning. A matrix of thinking
> skills and multiple intelligences can help you do this.

Content-based lessons benefit from the same variety and balance of
activity types and integrated skills as other lessons and, when carefully
planned and taught, are equally, if not more, engaging.

Let's consider, as an example, a content-based unit of work on bugs
with links to maths (counting the legs of bugs), science (classifying
bugs), art and craft (making a model of a bug), technology (researching
unusual bugs), literacy (reading a story about bugs), music (learning a
song about bugs) and drama (acting out the life cycle of a bug). Basic
subject vocabulary includes names of bugs (*butterfly, spider*, etc.), body
parts (*legs, wings*, etc.), actions (*fly, jump*, etc.), numbers and colours.
More advanced subject vocabulary includes additional body parts
(*antennae, thorax, abdomen*), actions (*slither*) and names for groups of
bugs (*insects, arachnids, gastropods, arthropods*). Language functions
enable children to describe, compare and classify bugs.

A matrix using Gardner's multiple intelligences and Bloom's revised
taxonomy of thinking skills is a practical, organisational tool to vary
activities and balance lower- and **higher-order thinking skills**. Examples in
relation to the unit of work on bugs are:

- Remember / visual spatial: flashcard activities to activate vocabulary;
- Understand / kinaesthetic: act out the life cycle of a bug;
- Apply / naturalist: picture cards to classify bugs into groups;
- Analyse / interpersonal: Sentence tennis (see **18**) comparing bugs;
- Evaluate / logical deductive: research to identify dangerous bugs;
- Create / verbal linguistic: invent a bug which belongs to a bug group.

Anderson, L. W. and Krathwohl, D. R. (2001). *A Taxonomy for Teaching, Learning and Assessing:
A revision of Bloom's Taxonomy of Educational Objectives.* New York, NY: Longman.

Gardner, H. (1983). *Frames of Mind: The Theory of Multiple Intelligences.* Fontana.

> One of the challenges of content-based teaching is to provide sufficient content and language support. There are a range of scaffolding strategies and techniques you can use.

Scaffolding is the term used to describe strategies and techniques which support children's learning. As the metaphor implies, scaffolding is temporary and can be put in place or withdrawn, according to children's needs. Scaffolding has an important role in content-based lessons where new concepts may be cognitively challenging and the language may not be graded.

Examples of scaffolding strategies and techniques you can use are:

- Activate prior knowledge: encourage children to connect previous and new knowledge (see also **16**). For example, get children to complete the K part of a KWLH grid (see **52**), or discuss true/false statements.
- Use visual techniques: use images, videos, web pages, **graphic organisers**, body language, gesture and mime to aid comprehension. Get children to use graphic organisers (see **52**) to record subject vocabulary.
- Use varied ways to show understanding: for example, get children to do a mime activity (see **65**) to show their understanding of vocabulary.
- Use **substitution tables**: give children substitution tables to support their speaking and writing.
- Use modelling: use **think aloud** procedures to **model** thinking processes that children can imitate.
- Repeat content in different ways: for example, present the same content in a text, a chart or a labelled picture.
- Use **discovery techniques**: such as problem-solving or hands-on activities to support understanding.

Last but not least, check understanding by getting children to provide evidence of what they know (see **6**) and be open to discussion of content concepts in the children's **shared language**, especially at initial stages.

Wood, D., Bruner, J. S. and Ross, G. (1976). 'The role of tutoring in problem-solving'. *Journal of Child Psychology and Psychiatry* 17(2), 89–100.

Adapt activities from other areas of the curriculum

> Even if you're not teaching CLIL, by adapting activities from other areas of the curriculum, you help to make language practice meaningful and memorable.

When children do activities that build on their knowledge of school subjects, they use English purposefully. This provides variety in practising grammar (see **X**) and increases children's interest and willingness to participate.

Two examples are:

1 Learning about plants – Seeds and stones

Language: *What's this? It's a … / What are these? They're …*; names of fruit, seed, stone

Preparation: Collect and dry seeds and stones from fruit, e.g. peaches, grapes, apples, plums, melons, apricots. Make sets of the seeds and stones (mixed together).

Activity: In groups, children sort the seeds and stones and identify the fruit, e.g. *What's this? (I think) it's a peach stone. / What are these? They're apple seeds.* Children then stick the seeds and stones on card and label them, e.g. *This is a plum stone. / These are melon seeds.*

2 Learning about animals – Animal groups

Language: *Does a mammal have warm blood? Yes, it does. / No, it doesn't. A mammal has / doesn't have fur*; names of animal groups and features.

Preparation: Give children a chart with the names of animal groups, e.g. *mammal, reptile, fish, bird*, and features, e.g. *fur, scales, wings, feathers.*

Activity: Children ask and answer questions, e.g. *Does a reptile have wings? Yes, it does. / No, it doesn't.* and complete the chart. Children do online research to check their answers. They then choose one animal group and write a description.

M: Thinking skills

The kinds of thinking skills that children need to develop at primary school include:

- **Cognitive skills**: for example, using deliberate memory, identifying and understanding relevant information, sorting, ordering, classifying, sequencing, comparing and contrasting, and linking cause and effect.
- Reasoning and enquiry skills: for example, justifying opinions, inferring, making deductions, asking relevant questions, anticipating problems and predicting **outcomes**.
- Creative and **critical thinking**: for example, critically evaluating things, generating and extending ideas, suggesting hypotheses and applying imagination.
- **Metacognitive** skills: for example, by reflecting on and evaluating learning and becoming aware of strategies for learning.

By integrating thinking skills in English lessons, children:

- extend and enrich their **language repertoire**;
- gain confidence in expressing their ideas;
- develop **communication strategies**;
- use language in ways that are personally meaningful;
- find lessons more interesting and challenging;
- learn skills which are potentially transferable;
- become more skilled at managing and evaluating their learning (see **17–19, 99** and **100**).

My key tips for thinking skills are:

49 Use questions effectively

50 Use every opportunity to promote thinking

51 Teach 'thinking language'

52 Use graphic organisers

49 Use questions effectively

> Questions probe and extend children's thinking. However, in order to be effective, you need to select questions with care and give children opportunities to ask their own questions.

Teachers are usually good at asking questions but often not so good at giving children time to reply or listening to the answers. Typical questions tend to be IRF (Initiation, Response, **Feedback**), e.g. *What colour's the bus? / Yellow. / Very good.* While these kinds of closed questions allow children to display knowledge and encourage participation, particularly in lower primary, they do not take thinking further.

Some examples of ways to extend children's thinking are by asking **probing questions** that: are open-ended and invite children to express their thoughts, e.g. *What do you like about …?*; encourage children to give reasons or evidence for their opinions, e.g. *Why do you think that? How do you know?*; get children to clarify or be more specific, e.g. *Can you give an example?*; encourage hypothetical or creative thinking, e.g. *What if …?*; develop **metacognitive** thinking, e.g. *How did … help you learn?*; promote enquiry skills, e.g. *How can we find out about …?*.

It helps to direct different types of questions to different children depending on their confidence and level of language and cognitive competence. If you understand the children's **shared language**, at times it will be appropriate to ask questions and/or accept responses in this too.

Children also develop thinking skills as much by asking relevant questions as by answering them. An example of an activity to develop this skill is Roll a question, played in pairs with dice made from coloured card with a different question word (*What? How? Why? When? Where? Who?*) on each face of the dice. After doing a topic or story, children take turns to roll the dice and ask their partner questions, using the question words on the dice.

Use every opportunity to promote thinking

> By actively promoting thinking, learning becomes more engaging and worthwhile. Many everyday classroom activities and procedures offer opportunities for this.

Children learn to think by thinking. As far as possible, you need to provide opportunities for children to think independently. This gives them **agency** and is empowering. One way is to offer children choice, for example, in activities or **outcomes** produced (see **37**). Another way is to conduct regular **learning reviews** (see **19**).

Other examples of activities which promote thinking are:

- Routines for thinking: at the start of a new topic, show children an image or give them true/false statements to discuss. This develops visual observation and/or reasoning skills. It also develops **metacognitive** skills by getting children to reflect on their current knowledge and to predict and anticipate what they will learn.
- Stories for thinking: stories develop thinking skills such as predicting, hypothesising, sequencing, deducing, reasoning, problem-solving and creative thinking. Stories offer an ideal opportunity for you to scaffold, or support, the development of children's thinking by asking structured questions that lead children to **recall**, comprehend, analyse and critically evaluate a story.
- Games for thinking: picture card games, such as Pelmanism, practise vocabulary recall as well as develop working memory and visual observation. Twenty questions gives children practice in asking *Yes/No* questions at the same time as developing analytical and logical deduction skills.
- Lateral thinking tasks and puzzles: these promote inventiveness and creativity. They also get children to listen with attention and develop deductive skills. For example, *A man rode into town on Monday. He stayed for three nights and then left on Monday. How come?* (*Monday* is the name of his horse.) (See also **81**.)

51 Teach 'thinking language'

> By teaching children 'thinking language', you help to make them explicitly aware of the processes involved in thinking. You also give them the tools to express their thoughts and ideas more effectively.

When teaching the youngest beginners, introduce three **chunks** of language early on: *I think it's … / Maybe it's … / I don't know.* Even with minimal other language, this gives children the opportunity to discuss things, for example, a partially visible flashcard: *I think it's a dog. / Maybe it's a horse. / I don't know.* You can then introduce: *I agree. / I don't agree.* and a bit later on: *Why? / Because … ,* so that children can also begin to give reasons for their opinions. By learning this kind of language, children feel motivated and empowered to express what they think in English. They also enjoy the structured turn-taking with other children.

Examples of 'thinking language' you may like to consider introducing include: verbs to express cognitive processes, such as: *think, know, guess, remember, predict, identify, compare, order, classify, research*; verbs to express perception, such as: *see, notice*; verbs to express personal preferences, such as: *like, love, prefer*; nouns for cognitive **outcomes,** such as: *survey, chart, diagram.*

In order to clarify the concepts behind 'thinking language', it's usually a good idea to **model** the thinking processes involved. For example, if you want children to make a comparison, you might say, *Let's compare rainforests and deserts. First of all, we need to think about what we know about rainforests and deserts. Then we need to identify the things that are similar and different. So, tell me what you know about deserts. / It's very hot. / It doesn't rain. / There aren't any trees. / Very good, and what about rainforests? / It's very hot. / It rains a lot. / There are tall trees. / Great. So what's similar and what's different? How can we compare them? We can say, for example, in rainforests and deserts it's very hot. It rains a lot in rainforests, but it doesn't rain in deserts.*

Use graphic organisers

Graphic organisers link learning to other areas of the curriculum and provide visual support for developing children's thinking and language skills.

Graphic organisers develop specific thinking processes and language. Bar charts enable children to count and compare figures, such as the results of a class survey. Venn diagrams help children identify similarities and differences, such as clothes to wear in summer and winter, or compare and contrast features, such as those of the North and South Poles. Concept maps enable children to identify elements of a topic and record vocabulary (see also **74**). Flow charts help children describe a process or the narrative sequence of a story. Choice boards present options for children to choose between (see **37** and **72**).

KWLH charts (where K = What I know, W = What I want to know, L = What I learnt and H = How I learnt it) develop **metacognitive** skills and provide a framework for self-directed project work (see also **18** and **37**). Placemats develop individual and collaborative thinking by getting children to note individual ideas before working together to share ideas and note what they collectively think are the main three.

It's important to choose graphic organisers that are in sync with children's **cognitive development**. For example, in order to read a bar chart, children need to understand the concept of coordinates. The first time you use a graphic organiser, it's best to build it up on the board with the whole class first, explicitly **modelling** and demonstrating the thinking processes and language involved.

With upper primary, graphic organisers also provide variety in developing reading and writing skills. For example, in a text comparing African and Asian elephants, children can note the similarities and differences in a Venn diagram, and a flow chart containing notes of a sequence of events can provide support for writing a story.

N: Vocabulary

For most children, learning new words is motivating and gives them a tangible sense of progress. It also supports their ability to interact and express personal meanings using a limited range of language **chunks** or grammatical structures.

However, learning vocabulary is more complex than it seems. Children need to recognise a word when spoken and **decode** it when written. They need to understand the meaning of the word and how it relates to other words, for example, the difference between *small* and *tiny*. They need to know how a word is used grammatically, for example, we say *she's a good swimmer* but not *she swims good*, and how it collocates with other words, for example, we say *a high mountain* but not *a high person*. Children need to be able to **recall** the word and know how to say it and spell it. Depending on their age, children also need to know the grammar of the word, for example, whether it is a noun or adjective, and be aware of register.

Children's vocabulary learning is influenced by their other languages and cultural background. As children develop greater maturity during the primary years, they also bring new understanding to vocabulary in English and this influences their learning too.

Children learn vocabulary through frequent, repeated exposure in meaningful contexts which allow opportunities for personal and social interaction and experiential use.

My key tips for vocabulary are:
53   **Move from concrete to abstract**
54   **Recycle frequently**
55   **Develop vocabulary learning strategies**
56   **Don't over-focus on spelling!**

Move from concrete to abstract 53

It's usual to teach concrete vocabulary first and leave more abstract vocabulary until children develop greater cognitive maturity. In either case, make sure that the meaning is clear and encourage children to notice the form.

Concrete vocabulary refers to items that relate closely to children's lives and that they can see, touch or act out in the immediate here and now of the classroom. Examples include classroom objects, food, actions and animals. Abstract vocabulary refers to items that are harder to illustrate and typically include more verbs, adjectives and adverbs than nouns.

When teaching vocabulary, you need to use appropriate ways to make sure that the meaning is clear. Examples of ways to do this are using visual and tactile means, such as flashcards and objects; physical means, such as mime; multi-sensory approaches, such as touching, pointing, walking to …; technology, such as apps, digital materials, videos; verbal means, such as defining the word and the context in which it is used; translation, for example, **eliciting** the meaning in the children's **shared language**.

In addition, you need to encourage children to notice the phonological form and written forms. For the phonological form, you can provide opportunities for children to listen to new vocabulary both in isolation (e.g. a flashcard game) and in a discourse context (e.g. a story); encourage children to repeat and experiment saying new words; draw attention to sounds, syllables and stress patterns (either implicitly or explicitly, depending on the age).

For the written form, you can provide opportunities for children to associate the written form with the sound and meaning; encourage children to notice the grammar of vocabulary; get children to copy and organise vocabulary carefully and accurately (see **55**).

54 Recycle frequently

Children need frequent opportunities to recycle vocabulary in multimodal activities and contexts. Recycling also includes opportunities for personalisation and creativity.

Through regular recycling, children develop their working memory and gain confidence in understanding and using vocabulary. They also build up a network of meanings that support their learning.

In lower primary, it helps to teach children **chunks** of language that they can use to **recycle** different lexical sets as you introduce them, for example, *I've got ... (a brother, a dog, a computer, brown hair, blue shoes) / I like ... (cheese, elephants, Maths, my friend, my sister, my hamster).*

As children learn new vocabulary, include this in your everyday, classroom communication whenever relevant. For example, once children learn to name pets or clothes, deliberately incorporate them into incidental, social classroom talk, e.g. *How's your cat, Lilian? / I like your T-shirt, Daniel.*

Establish a pattern whereby you do a short, recycling activity at the start of every lesson. This might be a flashcard game or other activity, such as Word tennis (see **25**), the Grid game (see **26**) or Circle time (see **30**). Other activities you can use to recycle vocabulary include stories, songs, chants, TPR (see **65**), mime and drama, crosswords, picture dictations, sorting, classifying and sequencing activities.

Recycling activities enable you to give personal relevance to learning. Examples are activities in which children relate vocabulary to their own feelings, opinions, beliefs, possessions, likes and dislikes. Creative recycling activities, such as writing a shape poem or designing a farm poster (see **37**), provide opportunities for children to use (even very limited) vocabulary in creative and diverse ways. Both personalisation and creativity make recycling of vocabulary memorable, give children **agency** and develop their ownership of learning.

> By introducing children to a wide range of vocabulary
> learning strategies, you help them to discover the ones they
> find most helpful.

Vocabulary **learning strategies** include **metacognitive** strategies, such
as self-testing in Look, cover, write, check (see **17**) and reflecting on
vocabulary **learning preferences** (see **18**). They also include the systematic
recording of vocabulary in notebooks, which can be organised in a variety
of ways, for example, in alphabetical order (with or without pictures and
translation), or according to topics, stories or units of work, and using
different formats such as lists, concept maps (see **52**), or collages. Other
vocabulary learning strategies are cognitive, such as using a dictionary
or categorising vocabulary into meaningful groups, and social, such as
describing an object to find out a word (see **18**) or asking for help.

Three examples of activities which integrate the development of
vocabulary learning strategies are:

- Magic eyes: stick a set of six to eight flashcards on the board. Point
  to the flashcards and children say the words rhythmically with you.
  Remove the flashcards in turn. Repeat the procedure each time,
  pointing to the flashcards as if they were still there. By the end,
  children are repeating all the words as you point to six to eight empty
  spaces. This activity gets children to use the strategy of associating
  pictures and words and develops their visual and working memory.
- Lip reading: stick a set of flashcards on the board. Choose one and
  mouth the word silently. Children read your lips and identify the
  word. This activity gets children to use the strategy of looking at
  people's lips to identify what they say.
- Teach a friend: prepare small picture cards (one for each child) of
  familiar vocabulary. Check children can **recall** and say their words.
  Children take turns to teach a partner their words. Once they are
  satisfied that they know the words, they swap cards and repeat
  the procedure with a new partner. This activity uses the strategy of
  teaching someone in order to remember and learn yourself.

56 Don't over-focus on spelling!

> **Accurate spelling is important, but you're more likely to achieve this if you keep the focus light.**

Children's spelling is influenced by their language background and how they are taught to spell in their mother tongue. It's also influenced by how much they read, or are exposed to written forms and whether they are taught **phonics** (see introduction to V). There may also be children with specific **learning differences** who find spelling challenging (see **71**).

Some children are naturally good at spelling: they have good visual memory and are willing to work out sound–letter correspondences and have a go. Other children are challenged by spelling and demotivated by the risk of getting it wrong. For this reason, it's important not to make an issue of spelling and to give children a lot of support.

Letter bags (bags with small alphabet cards) are a versatile resource. For example, get pairs to make words from a lexical set. Alternatively, dictate words and children use the alphabet cards to spell them. Children can also make anagrams of words and work out each other's words.

Other activities include Spelling gym (see **22**), which encourages children to memorise spellings through kinaesthetic association, and Kim's game with word cards (see **25**), which promotes visual memory of whole words. You can also organise Spelling bees in which children spell words and score points in teams.

With older children, spelling rules may be helpful, for example, add *es* to words ending in *x, ch, sh, s, z* to make plurals. You can also introduce spelling strategies, such as:

- Apply a letter pattern from a familiar word, e.g. *you* to other words with the same pattern, e.g. *could, should, would.*
- Use a mnemonic to help with letter order, such as *It's a great help!* for words with *gh* such as *fight, light, right, night, flight.*
- Create a sentence to memorise letter patterns, e.g. *Watch the match and catch the ball!*

O: Life skills

Life skills is an umbrella term that covers a wide range of personal, social and thinking skills. The overarching life skill addressed in this book is developing children's ability to communicate in a foreign language. Other life skills which relate to this include social and emotional learning (see, e.g. **G, J, 60, 66, 75**), **autonomy** and responsible decision-making (see, e.g. **8, J, 83**), learning how to learn (**E**), **values** education (**H**), **intercultural competence** (**K**) and thinking skills (**M**).

The aim of teaching life skills to children is to develop their awareness, understanding and practical ability to handle everyday life at home and school. Life skills help children to deal with the pressure of exams, and parents' expectations, develop positive **self-esteem** before the challenges of adolescence and develop soft skills such as the ability to work as part of a team.

Children learn life skills as appropriate to different ages. For example, life skills in lower primary might include learning to share with other children, whereas in upper primary, life skills might include learning how to stay safe on social media. The development of life skills is best integrated with other work in an active and experiential way. Classroom activities you can use for this include stories, songs, games, role play, problem-solving and **cooperative learning** activities.

My key tips for life skills are:

57 Promote children's wellbeing

58 Ensure safe and responsible use of technology

59 Raise awareness of social justice

60 Teach children presentation skills

57 Promote children's wellbeing

> Children's wellbeing impacts their learning, behaviour
> and ability to cope with life. You can contribute to this in
> many ways.

Wellbeing is a physical and mental state that enables children to feel
good about themselves. Children with a high level of wellbeing feel
safe, cared for, listened to and understood. They accomplish goals and
get positive **feedback** and praise. They eat well, sleep well, drink lots of
water and have frequent opportunities for play and exercise.

Although children's families are the main source of their wellbeing, you
have a significant role to play. This is reflected in your ability to develop
positive relationships (see **5**), **cooperative learning** (see, e.g **75**), effort,
resilience (see **32**) and **autonomy** in decision-making (see **8** and **37**) and
reflected in the way you manage children (see **10, 11** and **12**).

Practical activities to promote children's wellbeing include:

- Things that went well: At the end of the week, children write three
  things that went well for them on sticky notes and choose one to
  share with the class. This encourages children to focus on positive,
  rather than negative, aspects of their lives.
- Gratitude note: Explain the value of gratitude. Children choose a
  special person, such as a friend, teacher or member of their family,
  and write them a note saying thank you for the ways they help them.
  This encourages children to value their relationships with others.
- Mindfulness: Mindfulness is to do with focusing on the present
  moment. It can help calm children down and reduce anxiety. Many
  primary teachers have long used similar techniques, such as having
  quiet reflection times, doing breathing or visualisation activities, and
  using calming rhymes to develop concentration and settle children.
  My advice for using mindfulness in class is, first of all, to practise it
  yourself and, ideally, to get some training.

> Learning to use technology in a safe and responsible way
> is an essential life skill for all children. Your approach to
> this, in conjunction with a clear school policy and parental
> collaboration, is vital.

The ability to use technology and navigate online is an integral part of many primary children's schoolwork and personal lives. Most schools have strict acceptable-use internet policies and safety rules which you and children need to be aware of and operate within. These should be shared with parents so that they can reinforce them at home. You also need to communicate how children are using technology in English lessons and provide guidelines for home support.

Three practical ideas to promote safe and responsible use of technology are:

1 Technology poster: make a poster to reinforce key ideas, for example:

Treat people as in real life (i.e. show respect, no cyberbullying)
Explore safely (i.e. visit sites you're allowed to go to)
Create but never copy (i.e. don't steal anyone else's work)
Hide your personal information (i.e. keep your privacy)
Never chat to strangers (i.e. be wary as in real life)
Only open attachments you trust (i.e. be aware of spam and malware)
Look out for fake news and images (i.e. identify reliable sources)
Only post if you're sure (i.e. your digital footprint is permanent)
Go and speak to an adult if you're worried (this is not telling tales)
Your safety is the most important thing!

2 Discussion cards: prepare cards, e.g. *Mark is 12. He plays online games with people he doesn't know personally. One day he receives a message from one of them asking him to meet.* Children discuss this (potentially dangerous) situation and what Mark should do.

3 Technology Kim's game (see **25**): project images of a bug, footprint, magnifying glass, key, heart, stop sign, permanent marker handwritten text. At the end, explain that all the images relate to technology safety. Children work out the connections, e.g. key = keep personal information safe.

> By raising children's awareness of social justice, you
> integrate language, thinking and values education in a
> relevant and meaningful way.

Even young children can understand that everyone deserves to be
treated fairly. As children get older, their understanding of social
justice broadens to include concepts such as discrimination, prejudice,
stereotyping, and an awareness of issues related to rights (see **31**), race,
gender, age, education, poverty and mental or physical disability.

Social justice issues need to be contextually and culturally appropriate.
Examples of activities are:

- Toys: project images of different toys. Discuss toys intended for girls
  (dolls, soft toys / pink, violet) and for boys (construction, action toys
  / red, green). Ask children if boys and girls should have different toys
  and listen to their views.
- Jobs: name jobs in turn, e.g. *doctor, firefighter*. Ask children to draw
  a picture of each one. Use the results to discuss gender stereotyping.
- Bullying: explain the concept of bullying. Prepare eight to ten
  statements to describe actions such as: *laughing at someone's mistake
  / imitating someone's accent / kicking someone*. Children sort them
  according to whether or not they constitute bullying (they all do).
- Picturebooks: use these to introduce social justice issues in an
  engaging and memorable way, for example, *The day war came* (child
  refugees and education), *And Tango makes three* (family diversity).
- Videos and online activities and games: use social justice videos
  and activities as the basis of language lessons. See, for example, UN
  Global Goals, *The world's largest lesson*.

Davis, N. (2018). *The Day War Came*. London: Walker Books.

Richardson, J. and Parnell, P. (2005). *And Tango Makes Three*. New York: Simon and
Schuster.

Search: "UN Global Goals + The world's largest lesson + lesson plans".

> By teaching children presentation skills, you develop their
> ability to communicate clearly and confidently.

Presentation skills include the ability to i) prepare, organise and structure a short presentation, ii) deliver it in a way that makes it interesting and engaging, and iii) interact with the audience and answer questions.

With younger children, 'show and tell' activities provide a gentle introduction to practising presentation skills. For example, you might ask children to bring in a favourite photo and get them to take turns in Circle time (see **30**) to tell the class about it.

When teaching presentation skills to older children, get them to work in pairs or groups, especially at first. This helps shy children and takes less time as there are fewer presentations. Presentations may be based on content-based work or projects. You need to:

- Teach **functional language** to structure the presentation, for example, *First of all / Next / And then / Finally / In conclusion …*
- Set a time limit and maximum number of slides, e.g. three minutes, five slides.
- Give children a basic plan and model, for example: Introduction – why we like dolphins; Main part – where dolphins live, what they eat, how they communicate; Conclusion – why dolphins are amazing animals; Questions.
- Give guidelines for creating slides, e.g. key words and (non-copyright) images.
- Explain children mustn't read their presentation. Get them to prepare small cards with key words instead.
- Demonstrate the importance of eye contact, open body language and speaking clearly and confidently.
- Get children to practise before giving their presentations.

After the presentations, encourage constructive **peer assessment** by asking, e.g. *What did you like about the presentation? What could be better next time?* (See also **99**.)

P: Art, craft and design

Art, craft and design activities include creating things such as puppets, masks, comics or advertisements. They can be used in a variety of ways to practise vocabulary and grammar, play interactive games, and act out role plays and stories.

When you decide to do an art, craft and design activity, you need to assess how time-consuming and difficult to manage the activity will be and balance this against the potential benefits for learning. These include developing children's confidence and **self-esteem**, motivating them to use language for a purpose, and developing their social and thinking skills.

In order to be effective, you need to set up and manage art, craft and design activities carefully. You should prepare the language, establish learning **outcomes** (see **14**), **model** the process, and **monitor** activities (both for making the product and for using it).

Children usually get great satisfaction out of making and using art, craft and design activities in order to develop their language skills. By chance, I recently met a young woman I used to teach when she was a child. She told me that one of the things she vividly remembered was making an origami book (see **63**) – an anecdote that made me reflect that art, craft and design activities help to make learning memorable too.

My key tips for art, craft and design are:
61 Keep it simple!
62 Maximise language practice
63 Share the delight of home-made books
64 Create digital art and design

By keeping art, craft and design activities simple, even the youngest primary children can work independently. You also save valuable lesson time without losing the motivational and other learning benefits.

The most effective art, craft and design activities require easily available materials and take minimal time to make. This ensures that children can both make the product and use it purposefully in the same lesson.

Two examples of activities, based on nothing more complicated than rectangular strips of card, are:

1 Bookmark: children cut a strip of card (15 x 5 cm). They cut thin strips at one end to make tassels for their bookmark or, alternatively, stick on pieces of coloured wool. Children write a sentence on one or both sides of their bookmark, for example, *I like reading about … (bears)* or *I like reading … (fairy tales)*. Children illustrate their sentences and decorate their bookmark, using crayons, finger paints and sticky shapes. Children take turns to show each other their bookmarks and read their sentences. Alternatively, they play a guessing game based on their bookmarks: *Do you like reading adventure stories? Yes, I do. / No, I don't.* or move round the class asking questions to find a partner who likes reading the same as themselves. Children can then use their bookmarks with their coursebook or at home.

2 Four-faced dice: give out a template of a strip of card (16 x 4 cm) with a tab at one end and a dotted line every four centimetres, dividing the strip into four squares. Children cut the card, fold along the dotted lines and stick the tab to make a four-faced dice. Children draw one to four dots on their dice and use it to play a board game. Alternatively, they draw pictures of e.g. food, and do a role play by taking turns to roll the dice and ask, e.g. *Would you like a biscuit? Yes, please* (if they don't have a biscuit on their dice) / *No, thank you* (if they do). This dice can also be used to play Roll a question (see **49**). A four-faced dice is easier to make than one with six faces and also better to use in language board games which may only have 20 or so squares.

Art, craft and design activities offer a lot of potential for language practice and natural communication. You need to make the most of this at every stage.

Before children start an activity, show them a completed example and teach them vocabulary for the materials they will need. As you give instructions for the activity, **model** and demonstrate the procedure (see **63** for an example). This is an ideal opportunity for children to develop listening skills in a naturally contextualised and supported way (see **81**). As children are usually keen to do the activity, they listen with full attention. Be ready to repeat and answer questions as you do this.

Set a time limit and **monitor** the activity discreetly. Be ready to help or intervene if need be. However, the main benefit while children are making their art or craft, is that you have a golden opportunity to create moments of personal, one-to-one contact with individual children. Use these to praise, support, encourage, and show interest in what children are doing in a quiet, confidential way. Ask questions to check vocabulary, explore and extend their ideas, and find out their opinions. Bend down to the child's level as you do this, smile and use eye contact. Although you won't have time to interact with every child like this during the activity, keep a mental note of who you do speak to, so that over time you interact equally with everyone.

When children use their art or craft work in a language activity, this gives them a focus and purpose for speaking (see **7** and **28** for guidelines to set up and manage activities). The fact of using art and craft they have made in a speaking activity makes younger children, in particular, feel safe. It also boosts their confidence and encourages risk-taking.

After the activity, store children's work (with their names on) to be used again in other activities. Alternatively, make a class display or children take their work home to show and share with their families.

There are many ways of creating home-made books. These can be used for multiple purposes and provide a rich resource for learning.

Children invariably feel highly motivated when you get them to create a home-made book. Home-made books provide a framework for developing a range of language, cognitive and social skills.

Two examples of how to create and use home-made books are:

1 Zig-zag books: children make these by folding card backwards and forwards in equal sections (one A3 sheet cut lengthwise in four makes four books). They are particularly effective with lower primary. For example, children can create a zig-zag book about things they like. On each page they draw a picture and write, e.g. *I like bananas. / I like my cat.* Children complete their books in short periods over several lessons. They take turns to read their books in pairs and find out what they have in common. One of the delights of zig-zag books is that, when you turn the pages, they never end!

2 Origami books: these have eight pages, including the covers, and can be made from A3 or A4 paper. Explain and demonstrate this stage by stage:

Fold the paper in half down the centre. Open the paper. / Fold the paper in half the other way. / Now fold one half down, so the edge of the paper lines up with the fold. / Turn the paper over and repeat with the other half. / Cut a line in the centre of the paper (covering two folded sections). / Fold the paper in half. / Bring the sides round carefully to form a book.

Origami books can be used in numerous ways, for example, to write mini fact files related to content-based work (see **L**), personalised books on topics such as my family or a **learning review** (see **19**). One of the delights of origami books is how satisfyingly simple they are to make!

64 Create digital art and design

> Digital art and design activities are motivating and provide variety. However, you need to ensure they're used purposefully to develop children's language, thinking and social skills rather than as an end in themselves.

Digital art and design activities are best done in pairs within a set time limit. Before starting, you need to teach children **functional language** for using technology collaboratively, e.g. *Try clicking here! / Let's delete this!*

Some examples of freely available activities are:

- Street art: in this activity, children make their own street art or graffiti. Link the activity to the topic children are doing, such as climate change. In pairs children use the rollers, spray cans, stamps and stickers to create street art to raise awareness of climate issues. They then compare and discuss the impact of their art. Search for "children + games + street art".
- Design an advert: this activity develops children's consumer awareness and can be linked to, e.g. food or toys. In pairs, children design an advertisement for an invented product using the options of offers, images and headlines. They then look at each other's adverts, decide on three products they want to buy, have a class vote to find the most popular choices, and discuss the reasons. Search for "children + design + advert".
- Super action comic maker: this activity allows children to construct their own comic strip story, including images for places, objects, characters and speech bubbles. In pairs, children construct a story. They then tell their story to another pair and/or write their story. Search for "children + comic maker".
- Create your own picturebook: children make a digital picturebook using images of places, objects and animals, and a writing tool. Do an example with the whole class first. Children then create a book in pairs and take turns to show and share their stories. Search for "children + picturebook maker".

Q: Mime and drama

Mime and drama support and extend children's learning. Classroom activities and techniques include mime, movement and dance, action and drama games. Other activities involve acting out, re-telling or creating stories, improvisation and role play, developing voice techniques and multimedia drama. Mime and drama also underpin the preparation and rehearsal of class plays and other public performances for children's families and school.

When choosing mime and drama activities, you need to consider the space you have available, the effect on children (will it **stir or settle**?) and the implications for classroom management (see **C**). You need to **model** and demonstrate activities with conviction and show children that you are also willing to participate. Make sure you never get children to do activities which make them feel embarrassed or ridiculous (a consideration particularly with older children) and show that you value their participation, effort and cooperation more than their dramatic skills.

Through using mime and drama, children develop confidence and willingness to cooperate. Mime and drama activities provide opportunities for physical movement, reinforce meaning and help to make learning memorable. Some drama activities extend and develop children's imagination and promote creative and **critical thinking**, as for example, when children take on fictional roles and explore choices, dilemmas and human feelings in a safe and non-threatening way (see also **24**).

My key tips for mime and drama are:

65 Use mime to support understanding

66 Encourage playfulness and imagination

67 Use role play to explore ideas and issues

68 Make the most of that end-of-term play!

65 Use mime to support understanding

Mime is an invaluable tool to convey meaning and for children to show understanding. Use mime frequently to familiarise children with language and build their confidence.

TPR (Total Physical Response) is the name often given to activities that require children to listen and respond in a non-verbal way. The main benefit is to give children opportunities to listen and associate language with meaning and physical movement before using it themselves. Some examples of TPR and related activities are:

- Action songs and rhymes: children mime or do actions in response to songs and rhymes, for example, Incy Wincy Spider.
- Story mimes: children mime in response to key words, actions or characters, for example, in Goldilocks: *Daddy bear has a big bowl.*
- Gym sequences: children respond to instructions, e.g. *Touch your toes! Stretch your arms! Run on the spot.* Start with one or two actions and introduce others cumulatively.
- Content mimes: children mime the life cycle of a butterfly: *You're a tiny egg on a leaf. / Now you're a tiny caterpillar* (see **46**).
- Action mimes: Say: *You're a tiger! / You're playing a violin!* Children listen and respond. When you say *Stop!* they freeze in position.
- Walkabouts: mime going to, for example, the beach, rainforest, do actions and give a commentary: *Let's walk along the path. Oh dear, it's wet. Let's jump over the puddle.* Children listen and mime with you.
- Letter mimes: pairs from two teams take turns to come to you for a letter, for example, *H* and mime it (in upper case) to their team. The first team to get all the letters and arrange them in order to make a word, for example, *elephant*, wins.

Asher, J. (1969). 'The Total Physical Response Approach to Second Language Learning', *The Modern Language Journal*, Vol. 53, No. 1, 3–17.

Drama activities work most effectively when you encourage playfulness and imagination. You also need to ensure children feel confident about risk-taking and do not feel you are judging them.

Drama activities provide a framework to develop all aspects of children's communication skills. They also encourage children to work together towards a shared goal. In order to be successful, you need to create an atmosphere in which children are motivated to participate and in which **feedback** and correction of language is handled in a constructive and sensitive way (see **96**). In some cases, children may feel more confident if they prepare drama activities in writing first. Some examples are:

- Keep going!: in pairs, children talk to each other on a theme for one minute, e.g. *my daily routine*; *my favourite sport*; *food I like and don't like*; *what I did last weekend*. Children can write descriptions first but must not look at them during the activity. They can also use their **shared language** to keep going if need be.

- Improvisation with props: in groups, give children a situation, e.g. at the bus stop, in the supermarket, park or cinema and props, e.g. scarf, dark glasses, hat, shopping bag, wallet, umbrella. Children use the props to invent their roles and improvise a conversation. Children can write the conversation first but must not look at the script when they act it out to the class.

- Fairy tale objects: in groups, give children an object from a fairy tale, e.g. a small bowl (from Goldilocks), a dancing shoe (from Cinderella). Children create (and possibly write) a role play based on how the object came into their possession.

- Change the scene: build up a six-to-eight-line dialogue related to greeting a friend. Children practise the dialogue in pairs. Change the scene each time to, e.g. a noisy party, a hot desert, a boat on a rough sea, the top of a freezing cold mountain. Children change their voices and act out the dialogue accordingly.

67 Use role play to explore ideas and issues

> By using role play to explore ideas and issues, children
> learn to express their views and justify their opinions in
> a safe and structured way. However, you need to provide
> input and prepare language children will use first.

By doing role plays, children learn to listen to each other and take turns.
They also learn to express opinions, construct arguments and defend
and justify their point of view. One of the major benefits of role play
is that it gives children an opportunity to take on pretend roles and
discuss significant or sensitive ideas and issues without the pressure of
being themselves.

The **input** for role plays frequently comes from stories, as when children
adopt fictional roles in order to explore issues that go beyond the
story (see **24**). It also comes from listening and reading texts based on
cross-curricular content, social justice (see **59**) or **values** issues (see **31**),
particularly with older children.

An example of a flexible role play is Chat show. Take the role of the
Chat show host yourself with two to four (confident) children as invited
guests and the rest of the class as audience. Make sure children are
familiar with **functional language** you want to encourage them to use,
such as: *In my view, ... / I agree / don't agree that ... / I'd just like to
add that ...* . Give the guests role cards outlining different views on the
chosen topic, for example, homework (see **8**) or climate change, and
distribute a few question cards to the audience. Introduce the topic and
guests. Invite each guest to speak in turn based on their role card. Then
invite the audience to ask questions and debate the issue.

The advantage of taking the role of Chat show host yourself is that you can
orchestrate the role play, ask appropriate questions, and support children
in expressing their views. The role play works best if you do not step out
of role until the end when you thank the guests and audience for their
contributions. You may also like to film the role play for **feedback** later.

Make the most of that end-of-term play! 68

By approaching the preparation and rehearsal of an end-of-term play as a class project, you maximise the language and other benefits.

The best way to find a suitable play is to involve children in choosing it. Plays I have done over the years have all been based on favourite picture books, traditional tales, or coursebook stories chosen by children.

When writing the play, you need to ensure there are enough parts for everyone. This can be achieved by having several narrators, additional characters, or a chorus that performs songs or rhymes as part of the play.

It's usually best to rehearse the play over several weeks in short ten-minute periods towards the end of lessons. While some children rehearse, others make the programme, props and invitations, and design a poster. If possible, get parents to help with simple costumes for the play.

By approaching the play as a class project, even the youngest beginners have an opportunity to understand and use language naturally, for example, to:

- Negotiate parts: *What do you want to be? I want to be the … / Me too!*
- Memorise the script: *Once upon a time, …*
- Make props: *I'm making a mask. / My mask is green.*
- Rehearse: *Stand here. / Speak louder. / Look at everyone. / Say it again.*
- Plan costumes: *I've got a red cape. / I can wear black boots.*
- Make programmes: *Who's Ana? She's the mother.*
- Make invitations: *Come to our play on (day) at (time)!*
- Greet the audience: *Welcome to our play! Here's a programme!*

The **outcome** is a motivating, collaborative, language-rich experience for children and a rewarding one for you. Preparing a class play also provides tangible evidence of progress to children's parents and helps to positively reinforce the home–school link.

R: Inclusion and diversity

One of my most vivid experiences of inclusion and **diversity** relates to a six-year-old child (let's call him Alex) diagnosed with Autism Spectrum Disorder. I'd been forewarned that Alex wandered about around the classroom in his own world and advised that the recommended approach was to take no notice and carry on teaching. Although I found this hard, I got used to it and the class teacher, who always sat in on my lessons, told me she was pleased that Alex seemed happy and was not throwing tantrums.

One day, when teaching the song Five little, green frogs, I brought to class a glove puppet with a frog on each finger. For some reason, Alex was entranced by this puppet and, while the class did individual work, I got each frog to say hello to him in turn. It's hard to describe Alex's total concentration and pleasure in this simple game.

From that day on, I brought the frog puppet to class every lesson. Whenever there was an opportunity, I surreptitiously got the puppet out of my bag and Alex cautiously approached to start playing. This became a routine and, little by little, Alex's confidence and language grew. This experience taught me one of the most valuable lessons of my career: that every child has unique learning potential and that by being adaptable and willing to relate to the child's world, you can help them to realise this.

My key tips for inclusion and diversity are:
- **69 Create an inclusive learning climate**
- **70 Celebrate diverse identities in your classroom**
- **71 Keep informed about specific learning differences**
- **72 Differentiate instruction and tasks as appropriate**

> By creating an inclusive learning climate, you promote
> equity and ensure access to learning for all children. The
> best way to start is by reflecting on your own attitudes,
> values and behaviour.

An **inclusive** learning climate is one in which children feel a sense of
belonging and know that you believe in them and support them.

In order to create an inclusive learning climate, you need to:

- Engage in constant self-reflection: what's your attitude towards the
  children you teach? Do you detect any favouritism or prejudice
  towards children of different race, gender or ability? Do you treat
  them equally?
- Build positive relationships: work patiently at building good,
  working relationships with all children (see **5**). Encourage respect
  and positive interaction between children. Treat children as
  individuals rather than as a group to be controlled.
- Create a sense of community: for example, get the class to choose a
  name for themselves and regularly display their work.
- Watch your language: use inclusive language and avoid generalisations,
  stereotypical language or labelling children (see also **6**).
- Be responsive and adaptive: notice children's individual abilities and
  learning preferences and be flexible in adapting your approach.
- Focus on the positive: build on children's strengths and celebrate
  their progress and achievement.
- Have high expectations: children are likely to do better – and feel
  more valued – if you keep these high.

By striving to create an inclusive learning climate in this way, you show
that you value and support the contribution and participation of all
children, and this benefits everyone.

70 Celebrate diverse identities in your classroom

> By celebrating diversity, you teach children to value their own identities and the uniqueness of their peers. You also develop empathy, tolerance and respect.

In one primary school where I worked, there were children with specific learning needs and 26 different nationalities. The whole school was proud of its **diversity**, evident from a large world map and photos in the entrance hall showing 'where we're from' with speech bubbles saying 'hello' in different languages. It was clear that the explicit policy of inclusion and diversity, combined with the way staff provided a positive role model, conveying care, tolerance and respect, was key to its success.

By celebrating diverse identities in your classroom, children develop social skills and learn how to connect with other children. They also become open to different ways of thinking and learn to recognise the emptiness of stereotypes. When children feel valued, their behaviour tends to improve too.

Examples of practical ways to celebrate diversity include:

- Critically evaluate your teaching materials: for example, who features in the images? Does the content reflect children's realities? If not, use other resources to redress this (see below).
- Get to know children: observe their strengths, weaknesses and **learning preferences** and listen to what they say.
- Do activities to celebrate diversity: for example, play a version of Simon says, e.g. *Everyone who wears glasses, jump up and down! / Everyone who speaks more than two languages, tap your head!*
- Make children feel special: for example, have a weekly 'special child' slot in which a child shares a favourite photo and information about themselves, such as their country, culture and language(s), and other children say positive things about them.
- Use resources that reflect diversity: for example, use news stories about children from other countries or picturebooks that explore diversity and support understanding of social justice (see **59**).

Keep informed about specific learning differences

By keeping informed about specific learning differences, you feel confident about understanding children's needs and empowered to support their learning appropriately.

Specific **learning differences** cover a wide range of needs relating to **cognitive skills**, learning, sensory and physical skills, social, emotional and behavioural skills, communication and interaction. It is your duty to inform yourself as best you can about individual children's specific learning differences in order to be able to safeguard children and support their learning in an appropriate way.

Whenever possible, it is useful to talk to, and learn from, children's parents as well as other teachers. There are also publications and websites you may find helpful. However, you need to remember that it is not your role to diagnose children, which is the work of professionals, but rather to seek out advice on how best to adapt your practice in order to support their needs.

In order to support children with specific learning differences, as well as creating an **inclusive** climate (see **69**) and celebrating diverse identities (see **70**), it is advisable to:

- ensure the learning environment is attractive but not over-stimulating;
- set clear lesson objectives and **differentiate outcomes** and **success criteria** (see **14**);
- use simple language, divided into stages, for instructions (see **6**);
- include regular **classroom routines**;
- value all children's **multilingual identities** and don't insist on English;
- manage children's behaviour positively (see **10**);
- differentiate instruction and tasks as appropriate (see **72**);
- provide for different **learning preferences**;
- promote participation by all;
- give positive **feedback** and focus on achievement and success.

72 Differentiate instruction and tasks as appropriate

> The need to differentiate instruction and tasks is challenging. However, there are many practical ways to approach this.

Whatever the circumstances, it's important to make teaching and learning appropriate to individual children's needs. Here are some things you can do:

- Offer choice boards: these are **graphic organisers** (see **52**) with six or nine squares outlining options for activities relating to a topic, e.g. *Draw a picture of …* . Children choose one or more activity. Activities vary in terms of the level of challenge and skills required. Some children may do several activities in the time available; others may only do one and feel more comfortable if you direct their choice.
- **Differentiate** questions: grade questions according to children's abilities and needs (see **49**). Be aware that it may not be appropriate to ask some children questions in front of the class.
- Use KWLH grids (see **52**): use these to set up self-directed project work particularly for gifted and talented children.
- Vary **success criteria**: tailor these to make the level of challenge and resulting **output** and sense of achievement appropriate for all children (see **14**).
- Exploit digital materials: with a digital version of a coursebook, children can either listen, read, or read and listen to a text. They can also listen and repeat vocabulary at the same time as reading the words or not. Digital, adaptive activities, games and assessments also adjust tasks and progress to children's level, although these may not be appropriate for all children.
- Vary **input**: use text, images, audio, video, graphic organisers, to provide for different **learning preferences**. Be ready to present the same input in multiple ways.
- Vary groupings: for example, get children to support their peers. This provides an extra challenge and promotes positive **values**.
- Support output appropriately: for example, if you ask children to write a short text based on a model, they can: i) complete a text with gaps or pictures; ii) order sentences on cards and either stick the cards in order or copy the text; iii) create their own text.

S: Creativity

Creativity is to do with having fresh, divergent responses and ideas. When developing creativity with children, you need to:

- provide a stimulus such as a question, image, story, object or problem;
- be sure that children are emotionally engaged and motivated to achieve a particular creative **outcome**;
- give children an opportunity to play with ideas freely and spontaneously without judging their contributions;
- provide a clear framework and **model** or build up an example of a creative outcome with the whole class first;
- teach the necessary language, skills and strategies to achieve a creative goal;
- give constructive **feedback** and praise which focus on children's effort and develop a growth mindset (see **32**).

As well as developing children's creativity, you can also enhance your teaching if you think about your own creativity. This means using varied, imaginative approaches to make your lessons more engaging and effective. Although this involves an element of risk-taking, you're likely to be rewarded by children's positive response, as well as expanding your own repertoire of teaching ideas.

My key tips for creativity are:

73 **Be creative in small ways**

74 **Explore and play with ideas**

75 **Provide a stimulus, a framework and a purpose**

76 **Think about what you usually do – and do something different!**

73 | Be creative in small ways

> By adopting a creative approach to routine aspects of your everyday teaching, you make lessons enjoyable, enrich children's learning and encourage them to think creatively too.

When you **model** creativity in small ways on a regular basis, you establish a learning environment in which new or different ideas are valued. You also motivate children to think flexibly and be creative too. Some examples are:

- Lining up: by asking children to line up by age, height or month of their birthday, you give this routine activity a learning purpose and make it enjoyable. Once children have got the idea, they are likely to suggest others, e.g. lining up by colour of clothes or alphabetical order of names.

- Taking the register: turn this into a word association game, e.g.Teacher: *Rachid – Cinema!* / Rachid: *Film!*, or geography lesson by pre-assigning a country to each child and when you name this, they say the capital, e.g. *Morocco!* / *Rabat!* As with lining up, children are likely to suggest other ideas too, e.g. pre-assigning animals and naming the young or making the sound, e.g. *Lion!* / *Cub!* (*or Roar!*)

- Physical break: when children need to move, do a gym sequence, e.g. *Stretch your arms.* / *Touch your toes.* etc. Vary your instructions and the speed. Once children are familiar with the activity, invite confident children to lead it.

- Managing children: use creative ideas to manage behaviour, for example, a yellow and red card system as in football, or a 'noisometer' based on traffic lights: red = *Too loud!*, orange = *Turn the volume down!*, green = *Our quiet voices!*

- Marking work: be creative and consistent. For example, write two colour-coded comments at the end of children's work: pink = praise and positive comment; blue = how to get better. Children can also use the system to evaluate their own and peers' work (see **99**).

Explore and play with ideas

> By getting children to explore and play with ideas, they learn to use their imaginations and think about things from different points of view.

Exploring and playing with ideas underpin children's imaginative thinking and lead to creative **outcomes**. To be most effective, you need to create an atmosphere of mutual respect where divergent views are valued, and children feel they can take risks. It's also advisable to demonstrate the kind of thinking you wish to encourage or **model** the activity first. You also need to be ready to support and **recast** children's contributions and accept and re-interpret ideas they may need to express in their **shared language**, with the help of other children if necessary.

Two flexible techniques that encourage children to explore and play with ideas are:

1 Concept maps (see **52**): use variations of these to explore a topic, solve a problem, prepare for a project, write a description or story. For example, a concept map with *Wh-* questions (*What? Why? When? How? Where? Who?*) guides children in formulating questions before doing a project, for example: *The moon: What is the moon made of?* A concept map with the five senses (see, hear, smell, touch, taste) **elicits** imaginative responses in preparation for a poem or description, for example: *The forest: I see tall trees.* A concept map with feelings (angry, afraid, surprised, hopeful, happy, sad) supports children in expressing how they feel about a particular issue, for example: *Climate change: I'm angry people don't care.*

2 *What if ...?*: This activity promotes imaginative, hypothetical thinking and can be used to explore children's creative ideas on any issue, topic or story, for example, *What if children ruled the world?* If you're concerned about children using the conditional tense, e.g. (*I think*) *they would stop wars,* you can re-formulate the question, for example: *Imagine children rule the world. What happens?*

75 Provide a stimulus, a framework and a purpose

> In order to support children's creative efforts, you need to provide a motivating stimulus, a clear framework and a relevant purpose.

There's nothing more frustrating for children than not having the language or skills to express their ideas or structure their work. For this reason, it's important to set up activities in a way that supports children's creative thinking and gives them the tools to succeed.

Two examples of **cooperative learning** activities which do this are:
1   Adventure
    Stimulus: Children listen to or read about an adventure.
    Framework: In groups, children imagine they had an adventure. Use a set of 10–12 word cards with past tense verbs, e.g. *went, saw*, and some blank cards. Children take turns to say a sentence and build up a creative account of their adventure. They lay the verb cards in order as they do this, and use the blank cards for alternative verbs, if they wish. Children then use the verb cards as prompts to write sentences describing their adventure. They work collaboratively to combine sentences and use adjectives to make their adventure more interesting.
    Purpose: Children take turns to recount their adventures to the class and decide which one is best.
2   Nature poem
    Stimulus: Interesting natural objects, e.g. shells, pebbles, rocks.
    Framework: In pairs, give children an object to touch and look at. Project a series of questions, for example:

Where do you find it? / What size, shape and colour is it? / How does it feel when you touch it? / What other words describe it? / What does it make you think of? / How does it make you feel?

Children answer the questions and create a poem about their object.
Purpose: Children create a class book of their poems.

Think about what you usually do – and do something different!

> One way to come up with fresh, imaginative teaching ideas
> is to reflect on techniques and procedures that you usually
> use and then do something different.

By deliberately varying your teaching procedures and techniques, you add interest to lessons and make them more dynamic. The principle of changing what you do can be applied to all areas of your teaching. There are frequently benefits in terms of children's creative responses too.

One example might be if, when teaching a story, you usually ask children to predict what happens from the cover or picture at the beginning, why not try using a picture from the middle of the story instead? In this case, you can divide the class into two groups: one group hypothesises what happens before the picture, and the other group hypothesises what happens afterwards. The groups take turns to share their ideas and see if they cohere as a story, before listening to the original and comparing it with their predictions. This activity develops children's imagination and ability to interpret a picture. It also creates a motivating purpose for listening.

Another example might be if you usually use 'odd one out' as a test item with only one right answer, why not try using it as a creative thinking activity instead? For example, show children four to five flashcards and children invent their own reasons for which is the odd one out. For example, from a set of animals: cat, mouse, turtle, bird, children might say: *I think it's 'mouse' because 'mouse' is part of a computer. / I think it's 'turtle' because 'turtle' is a reptile.* This activity gets children to think flexibly and motivates them to justify their ideas.

A third example might be if you usually ask children *Wh-* questions after a reading text in order to check comprehension, why not get them to formulate questions instead to check each other's – or yours? This motivates children to read the text with attention as they usually want to ask questions that are as challenging as possible. It also gives children useful practice in asking questions too.

T: Adapting or writing materials

Your materials need to be as well suited as possible to your classes and teaching context. There are, therefore, bound to be moments when you need to adapt or write them yourself.

Whether you are looking to evaluate materials to use, or to design and write them yourself, you need to keep in mind that the most effective materials for children:

- provide natural, meaningful exposure to language;
- take account of all aspects of children's development;
- engage children cognitively and affectively;
- focus on meaning before form;
- develop discourse skills, not just single words or **chunks**;
- are **inclusive** and take into account **learning differences**;
- promote purposeful participation and communication;
- provide a variety and balance of experiential activities;
- personalise learning;
- offer choice and encourage independence;
- provide a suitable level of challenge (see Vygotsky's **Zone of Proximal Development** (ZPD) or the 'Goldilocks rule' – not too easy, not too difficult but just right);
- provide support to ensure the challenge is achievable;
- promote learner independence;
- provide varied, appealing modes of **input** and practice;
- incorporate educational issues such as social and emotional learning, **values** and **life skills**.

My key tips for adapting or writing materials are:

77 **Don't be a slave to the coursebook!**

78 **Collect additional materials and resources**

79 **Adapt your approach to cater for mixed age groups**

80 **Design and write the course yourself – but think twice first!**

Vygotsky, L. S. (1978). *Mind in society: The development of higher psychological processes.* Cambridge, MA: Harvard University Press.

Don't be a slave to the coursebook!

> Your coursebook is an invaluable teaching and learning resource. However, you need to keep a critical mindset and modify or extend it as necessary to meet the needs and interests of children.

If you're a busy, full-time teacher, there's no doubt that a coursebook can save your life. All the organisation of materials and sequencing of language is done for you, and you can get by with minimal preparation if need be. At the same time, there are ways in which it may be beneficial to make changes to your coursebook. These include:

- **Learning differences**: adapt activities to support these (see **72**).
- Use of images: images may not be representative or culturally appropriate, or they may be attractive but not actively exploited. Be ready to provide a balance (see below).
- Practice activities: these may be highly controlled, never giving children an opportunity to take risks. Find ways to extend them, for example, by incorporating activities that go beyond stories (see **24**).
- Approach to grammar: this may be repetitive and dull. Find ways to make grammar practice purposeful, for example, through content-based activities (see **48**) or information gap games (see **95**).
- Educational **values**: a coursebook based on structural progression may not include broader educational issues. Find ways to include these, for example, values that derive from a story (see **31**).
- Balance: redress any imbalance in skills development or coursebook characters, for example, by using more varied images and texts and picturebooks which reflect **diversity**.
- **Learning reviews**: these may be inadequate. Introduce them regularly (see **19**) to ensure the development of learner **autonomy** and **metacognitive** skills.
- Assessment: this may be only based on tests. If so, look to extend and enrich the assessment programme (see **97–100**).

78 Collect additional materials and resources

> By building up a bank of additional materials and resources, you add variety to lessons and enrich learning. However, additional materials should always be used with a clear learning intention and not for the novelty value alone.

The best additional materials and resources are ones that engage children and can be used flexibly with different classes. Your collection may include resources that you make yourself, such as class sets of jumbled sentences (see 8), word cards (see 75) or board games (see 27).

The time, effort and expense that you invest in making resources yourself, makes it worth ensuring they are durable, for example, by laminating cards and writing numbers on the reverse side to identify class sets. You also need to create a reliable filing system, including electronic files and bookmarking for digital materials and resources, and clearly labelled folders and storage boxes for physical ones.

Three examples of flexible, additional materials and resources are:

1 Poems: there are many poems for children on everyday themes that are accessible and engaging (see, for example, the works of Roger McGough and Michael Rosen). Poetry provides exposure to authentic language and to humour. You can use poems to develop skills in a similar way to stories (see 23) and other reading texts (see 88), or introduce 'a poem a month' as part of reading for pleasure (see 86).
2 Postcards: sets of postcards showing works of art, capital cities or famous monuments provide a highly versatile resource. Use them to develop **visual literacy** (see 90), for **content-based learning** (geography or art), descriptive writing, or as the basis of guessing games, rank ordering activities or getting children to express personal preferences.
3 Publicity leaflets: these may be for events, such as concerts or theatre, or products, such as toys. Use them to develop children's ability to scan and find information such as price and to do **cooperative learning** activities such as selecting toys within a budget for a children's charity.

> Working with mixed age groups is undoubtedly a challenge. However, there are many ways you can adapt your approach and turn it into a positive and rewarding experience.

Although you need to plan and organise lessons with extra care, there are benefits to working with mixed age groups. Younger children enjoy learning knowledge and skills from older children. Older children gain from teaching younger ones and develop responsibility and empathy.

Some ways you can cater for mixed age groups are:

- Use flexible resources: for example, use postcards as outlined in **78** or for vocabulary practice with younger children.
- Develop skills appropriately: for example, older children can read a picturebook to younger children. As follow-up, younger children do comprehension activities (see **23**) and older children create a parallel story.
- Use the same topic or theme: and **differentiate** learning **outcomes** and **success criteria** appropriately (see **14**).
- Use inquiry-based learning: pose a question such as *How are animals different?* and differentiate the level and age-appropriacy of investigative work for children to answer.
- Provide age-specific materials and task: get children to work in age sets and train them to expect that you will divide the time and support you give to each set.
- Make the most of technology: use apps and websites that are suitable for different age groups.
- Vary groupings: children work in age sets or mixed age sets depending on the activity. However, bear in mind that it may be frustrating for older children to work with younger ones for long.
- Set up a buddy system: organise pairs of older and younger children to learn from and support each other at suitable moments.
- Use plenary time at the end of lessons: get older and younger children to report, review and share what they have done. This brings the class together and reinforces a sense of community.

80 Design and write the course yourself – but think twice first!

> Given that you know your learners best, it may be tempting to design and write the course yourself. However, don't underestimate the time and effort involved!

The main appeal of designing and writing a course yourself is that you can tailor it to children's interests and needs. However, the main challenge lies in planning and producing a syllabus, materials and assessment tools that are visually attractive and varied, and have the logical progression and overall coherence of a course. You also need to ensure that you avoid photocopying materials for children from sources that may infringe copyright.

It helps if you collaborate with colleagues to plan the course and divide the work. It's also beneficial to build in a system of evaluation and review both before and after using the materials.

Two possible options are:

1 A story-based course: this involves selecting suitable children's picturebooks on relevant themes and deciding how much contact time to spend on each one. You need to analyse the language, set learning objectives, write materials for each story (see F) based on **learning cycles** with clear **outcomes** and **success criteria** (see D), and devise ways to assess learning (see Y). There are examples of using picturebooks as the basis of modules of work freely available online to help.

2 A theme-based course: an example for upper primary is a course based on the UN's 17 Sustainable Development Goals (SDGs) and freely available, educational materials online. You need to select goals to form the basis of your course and plan topics for each one. You also need to specify learning objectives, possible outcomes, **cognitive skills**, language, vocabulary, **values** and **life skills** for each one.

Search: "picturebooks + primary ELT teaching materials"; search: "SDGs + educational resources"

U: Listening and speaking

Listening and speaking are crucial in developing children's skills as effective communicators and underpin their **self-esteem** and social development. Listening and speaking also have a significant impact on the development of literacy skills and children's ability to read and write.

As in their mother tongue, children develop listening skills ahead of learning to speak. Through listening to English, children are drawn into speaking and gradually move from using single words and **chunks** to learning how to express their ideas and interact in a more sustained way.

The key to developing listening skills is to provide frequent, varied opportunities to listen to language in engaging and meaningful contexts, and to support this in an appropriate way. There are many examples of listening activities in previous sections of this book, such as Storytelling (**F**), Playing games (**G**), Songs, rhymes, chants and raps (**I**). However, the person most likely to provide the main listening **input** through everyday classroom talk and routines, giving instructions and explanations, managing children, giving **feedback** and praise and conducting **learning reviews**, is *you*.

Although children usually learn to speak English rapidly in immersion contexts, it is important not to underestimate the difficulty in contexts where they have two or three lessons per week. Above all, it is important not to make children speak before they feel ready to do so, and to accept **translanguaging** by responding positively to children's meaning.

My key tips for listening and speaking are:

81 **Support listening appropriately**

82 **Repeat, rehearse, recall**

83 **Provide opportunities for creative expression**

84 **Develop pronunciation skills**

81 Support listening appropriately

> In order to support listening appropriately, you need
> to develop children's attention skills and guide their
> understanding. You also need to be a good role model of
> active listening yourself.

- Be a good role model: a good listener is someone who looks at the speaker, stays focused, doesn't interrupt and responds respectfully. When you **model** active listening, you also convey that you are interested in listening to children and this encourages them to speak.
- Develop attention skills: children often have short concentration spans which make it difficult for them to listen with attention. For this reason, it can be invaluable to do short listening activities that progressively develop children's ability to focus and concentrate. One example is TPR activities (see **65**): children listen and follow instructions, e.g. *Jump three times!* (See also, e.g. **43** and **61**.) Another example is dictation: give short dictations such as a lateral thinking puzzle (see **50**), which children then solve, or a picture dictation in which children listen, draw and colour what you describe.
- Guide children's understanding: when children listen, they construct meaning from all the clues available: the language, the context, their knowledge of the world, their expectations of the speaker's intentions, and the speaker's use of facial expression, gesture and voice. Other factors such as their predictions, their reason and purpose for listening, and features, such as flashcards, coursebook or story illustrations, objects, puppets or sound effects, also support their understanding.

It's helpful to use a three-stage plan including pre-, while and post-listening activities to develop children's ability to make the most of all these clues.

These 3 Rs develop children's working memory and build confidence in speaking. It's best to integrate them regularly into lessons in ways that are playful and purposeful.

The ability to **recall** is essential in learning to speak a foreign language. In the case of young children, who are in the process of developing their deliberate memory, it also needs plenty of practice. Through repetition, children become familiar with different combinations of sounds attached to new meanings. This helps them memorise vocabulary and **chunks** of language, and acquire pronunciation in a natural, non-threatening way.

There can, however, be nothing more boring for children than repeating language for its own sake. Some ideas to make this playful and purposeful include:

- Flashcard games: in It's my word! for example, stick four to six flashcards on the left of the board for one team and four to six flashcards on the right for the other team. Say the words in random order. Children stand up, point to and repeat the word if it belongs to their team. (See also **55**.)
- True/false games: say sentences that are true and false related to language children are practising, e.g. *Birds can fly!* Children do actions to show their understanding and repeat the sentences if they are true.
- **Cumulative** games: in groups, children take turns to contribute sentences and repeat them cumulatively, e.g. *He likes strawberries, she likes pears, I like apples,* etc.

In addition to repetition, it's beneficial to give children regular opportunities to rehearse language with peers before using it with the whole class. This makes them feel secure, more willing to take risks, and their confidence grows. Rehearsal is suitable if children are preparing a role play or creating a dialogue to perform to the class. In **think-pair-share** activities, rehearsal also gives children an opportunity to formulate and express their ideas with a partner before sharing them publicly.

83 Provide opportunities for creative expression

Creative expression, such as in free play, gives children a chance to use their whole language repertoire in imaginative ways. However, you need to plan and prepare for this with care.

Free play contrasts with playing games which have rules and goals (see **G**). The best way to prepare children to engage in free play in English is to make the most of the 3 Rs (see **82**). Use these to develop children's familiarity with interactive exchanges on everyday themes, as well as teaching and learning routines, such as playing flashcard games. In this way, you create models, or 'formats', which provide the support, or **scaffolding**, children need, to subsequently improvise and create their own versions.

A feasible way to give lower primary children opportunities for free play is to set up learning stations. Learning stations engage children in using language they know in meaningful, self-directed ways and develop **autonomy**, responsible decision-making and cooperation. Learning stations also give you the chance to give extra support to small groups of children in turn. Children take turns to work at their desks and visit the stations in pairs or small groups. Each learning station has a resource to prompt interaction and free play, such as the class puppet and flashcards. Children play with the resources in any way they like. In my experience, a favourite learning station activity is pretending to be the teacher!

With older children, it's also important to prepare for self-directed speaking activities that offer the possibility of creative expression. For example, children listen to and practise a dialogue, *Guess what happened to me yesterday!* before improvising their own creative versions. Alternatively, introduce **functional language** to support children in freely exchanging views on topical issues or doing cooperative problem-solving activities.

'A format is a routinized and repeated interaction in which an adult and child do things to and with each other.' Bruner, J. (1983). *Child's Talk: Learning to use Language*. NY: Norton.

Young children acquire pronunciation naturally through exposure, repetition and imitation. As they get older, it's helpful to raise their awareness of specific features of pronunciation too.

In lower primary, a global approach to pronunciation exposes children to language through classroom talk, stories, songs, games and other activities, and is likely to be the most effective. As children mature, however, it's often appropriate to do activities that raise awareness of features of pronunciation such as sounds, stress, rhythm and intonation. It makes sense to focus on features that may be different in the children's language or cause particular difficulties. For children learning to read and possibly doing **phonics** (see introduction to V), it may also be appropriate to do activities that develop their awareness of sound–spelling correspondences.

Examples of pronunciation activities are:

- Tongue twisters: these provide an enjoyable way to practise individual sounds. You can easily invent your own, e.g. *Hannah is happy to help at home in the holidays*. In pairs, children see how many times they can say the tongue twister in 30 seconds. You can also teach children tongue twisters as fun passwords to, e.g. turn on computers or open the class cupboard.
- Sound categories: these are activities to practise discriminating sounds. For example, in *Cheese or chicken?*, say familiar words in random order with /ɪ/ or /iː/. Children jump in the air, put their arms by their sides and make themselves as thin as possible for words with /ɪ/, or jump in the air and stretch out their arms and legs to make themselves as wide as possible for words with /iː/. Children then sort the words and notice the spelling patterns.
- Recognising stress: children identify and clap the main stress in familiar words, e.g. *banana, Monday*, or in sentences or questions from stories, dialogues, rhymes or chants, e.g. *What's the time?*

V: Reading and writing

Both reading and writing involve an interaction of bottom-up and top-down skills. Bottom-up skills for reading include recognising letter shapes and knowing sound–spelling relationships. For writing, they include the motor skills involved in forming letters, and an ability to spell and use punctuation. Top-down reading skills include knowledge of different text types and how they are organised, as well as using graphic content and background knowledge to help construct meaning. Top-down writing skills include knowing how to apply awareness of audience, style, genre and register in order to communicate meaning.

There are no right answers about when to introduce reading and writing in English. This depends on the age, context, number of teaching hours, language background of children and the approach to literacy in the mother tongue.

In some contexts, early foreign language programmes include **phonics**. Although phonics can be helpful, there is a 'health warning'. Most children learning English as a foreign language do not have the extensive vocabulary that phonics assumes in order to be able to identify patterns across words. There is also a danger of children being taught words because of their form rather than what they mean. If you do include a focus on phonics, it is advisable to make sure that children use the language in meaningful contexts first.

My key tips for reading and writing are:
85 Share and model the process
86 Encourage reading for pleasure
87 Don't make writing a chore and a bore!
88 Use reading to support writing

> By sharing and modelling the processes of reading and writing, you support children in learning to read and write independently.

Shared reading is a technique that can be used at any age or level. Big books or texts projected on screen are particularly suitable. The objective is to read a text aloud *with* children, rather than *to* children, and to scaffold interaction in order to collaboratively construct meaning and comprehend the text. As you read, encourage participation and ask questions to build up understanding of the content, language, structure and organisation, including features that you wish children to notice, such as onomatopoeia, alliteration or repetition in a story. Talk through strategies that help children to **decode** and make sense of the text, for example, predicting words, or noticing pronominal reference. Encourage children to express personal responses to the text and give reasons. With older children, you can also use shared reading to raise awareness of style and register, and develop an understanding of inference and **critical literacy** (see **92**).

It isn't usually advisable to get children to take turns to read a text aloud around the class. Reading aloud is a demanding skill which involves scanning ahead to make sense of phrases and sentences and children may not be easily audible or intelligible. While one child reads, there is also little motivation for others to listen, leading to possible management problems.

Shared writing is a technique in which children collaboratively create a written text. For example, in response to watching a video on elephants, use children's contributions to collectively build up a description of elephants on the board. As children construct the text, ask questions to support their writing, e.g. *Shall we repeat 'elephants' here? What can we say instead? / They ... / Great!* At the end, read the description you have constructed together and get children to notice features, such as the use of pronouns and connectors, that make it function as a written text. As a follow-up, children independently write a description of another animal of their choice using the text you have created together as a model.

86 Encourage reading for pleasure

> Encouraging reading for pleasure means doing just that – free choice over what to read, no pressure and no obligatory worksheets. Start young and notice children blossom both as people and as learners!

Children become better readers by reading. They also develop their vocabulary and become better writers. Through reading for pleasure, children develop increased motivation, confidence and **autonomy**. They also develop their knowledge of the world, **visual literacy**, enhanced thinking skills, such as problem-solving and **critical thinking**, and social and emotional skills, such as empathy.

Some things to keep in mind when incorporating reading for pleasure are:

- Set up a regular time when children choose books. Make this into a pleasant routine. Never impose choices but be ready to help, if asked.
- Don't worry if children choose books above or below their level. Over time, they will find out what suits them. With young children, it's also fine if they mainly look at the pictures. It's their enthusiasm that counts.
- Get children to keep a record of books they read, possibly with a star system to show how much they like the book or would recommend it to friends.
- Show interest in children's reading but don't make reading competitive or part of a **reward system**. It is children's intrinsic motivation to read that counts.
- Set aside regular ten-minute slots in lessons for ERIC (Everyone Reading In Class). This also gives you an opportunity to **model** your own enthusiasm for reading.
- Inform parents about your reading for pleasure programme and how they can support this at home.

Don't make writing a chore and a bore!

> In order to sustain children's motivation in learning to write, it's important to make it enjoyable, meaningful and purposeful from the start.

Initial writing consolidates oral/aural work. It also supports the development of initial reading skills. Activities often include copying or completing words or short sentences. However, if over-used, they soon become boring and risk losing children's interest and motivation.

Some ways to make initial writing activities engaging are to include:

- Thinking skills: for example, children classify familiar vocabulary of things to buy, such as *ball, apple, shirt*, by copying the words into frames of the correct shops (*toy shop, supermarket, clothes shop*).
- Personalisation: for example, children categorise familiar vocabulary into items they like / don't like by copying the words into two lists.
- Visual observation: for example, children spot the differences between two pictures and write or complete sentences comparing them.
- A game: for example, children choose six words from a familiar lexical set, and write each one on pieces of paper. When they are ready, play Bingo! and children turn over the papers when you call their words.

As children get older and more competent, it is equally important to ensure that writing is not perceived as a chore and a bore. You always need to ask yourself how writing activities are taking children's learning further. If the answer is that they're only keeping children busy or quiet, then the value is questionable. Ideas for making writing motivating, engaging and worthwhile include collaborative writing (see **27, 75, 88**), content-based writing (see **46, 48, 63**), personal writing (see **2, 23**), descriptive writing (see **74**), creative writing (see **33, 63, 66**), preparing presentations (see **60**), poetry writing (see **75**) and projects (see **J**).

88 Use reading to support writing

> By using reading to support writing, children become
> aware of different goals and strategies for reading
> and writing. You need to give them plenty of varied
> opportunities to practise their skills.

As well as coursebook texts, you can use other authentic materials, such
as picturebooks and webpages. You also need to vary tasks beyond
standard ones, such as *Wh-* questions, true/false statements, or gap-
fills, and give children opportunities to express their personal views. It
is often effective to plan sequences of work that mirror the processes
of reading and writing, and integrate these with listening, speaking,
thinking and social skills. The following is an example based on blurbs,
or short descriptions, on the back of books:

1. Ask children what types of books they like, e.g. adventure stories.
2. Introduce the concept of a blurb. Show an example and do a
   shared reading activity (see **85**). **Elicit** children's ideas about the
   purpose, the audience and language of blurbs.
3. Give pairs a copy of a blurb and a strip of paper.
4. Children read the blurb and i) identify the type of book, ii) invent
   a title and write it on the strip of paper.
5. Collect in the titles and blurbs. Display the blurbs.
6. Re-distribute the titles. Children walk round the class, read the
   blurbs and identify the one that matches their title.
7. Children report back. They compare the invented and real titles
   and say if the blurb makes them interested in reading the book.
8. Give out strips of paper with different book titles. Establish **success
   criteria** (see **14**) and children work in groups to write a short blurb.
9. Display the titles and blurbs together.
10. Children choose the book they want to read and say why.

This sequence makes children aware of the value of reading blurbs
when selecting books and of features they can use in their writing, such
as adjectives and ellipsis, to make it interesting and persuasive.

W: Multiliteracies

Multiliteracies refer to understanding and communicating meaning in multiple modes. They form an integral part of children's emotional, psychological, social and **cognitive development** both at home and at school. They also enrich and extend children's language and communication skills.

Multiliteracies involve supporting children in constructing and creating meaning from non-linear, **multimodal texts**, including print, images, graphics, audio, film and music. Through multiliteracies, you can also introduce children to **critical literacy**.

By using multiliteracies in your everyday teaching, you are likely to make a significant and motivating contribution to the development of children's basic literacy skills. The opportunity to use digital, multimodal means to do things such as listen to podcasts, watch videos, play games, do research, create projects, stories or presentations in English lessons, provides a purposeful and enjoyable context for children to apply and practise their skills.

However, for some children, multiliteracy activities may be a source of distraction or confusion. You therefore need to plan carefully to ensure that they are neither over-stimulating nor over-long, and that children have appropriate learning support. You also need to keep a healthy balance between screen and face-to-face time in order to sustain everyone's interest over the longer term.

My key tips for multiliteracies are:

89 Integrate digital media and technology

90 Develop visual literacy

91 Use multimodal texts to enrich learning

92 Lay the foundations of critical literacy

89 | Integrate digital media and technology

> By using digital media and technology tools, as available
> and appropriate, you provide variety and enrich learning.

Working with digital media and technology is standard in many
contexts. For children, this offers the opportunity to work
independently and develop **digital literacy** skills, such as researching,
creating content and collaborating online. At the same time, children's
online safety is crucial (see **58**). You also need to be aware of the
potential impact of screen time on children's attention skills, physical
and mental health. This means balancing the use of digital media and
technology with face-to-face communication, physical movement and
experiential learning in class. A key question to always ask yourself
when planning to use digital media and technology is: what is the
learning benefit of doing it this way?

As well as online activities and games (see **59**), art and design (see **64**),
creating projects (see **37**) and presentations (see **60**), examples include:

- Interactive voting, quizzes and polls: applications allow you to create
  quizzes, get children to express preferences, or evaluate how well
  they have done. Search: "primary teaching + interactive voting".
- Blogs: personal and class blogs are a motivating and engaging
  way of getting children to record, share and contribute ideas and
  opinions. Use sites to create blogs which you can **monitor** and keep
  private. Search: "primary education + creating blogs".
- Creating videos: this is an enjoyable, collaborative activity which
  develops language, thinking and social skills. Some apps also allow
  children to upload their own drawings or photos into their videos.
  Search: "primary education + creating videos".
- Digital storytelling: use apps to engage children in creating their own
  stories. Search: "primary education + creating digital stories".

> Through developing visual literacy, children learn to
> construct meaning from images. This supports their
> language learning and ability to think critically about
> images in the real and digital world.

Children grow up in a world with visual images everywhere: films,
photos, advertisements, webpages, picturebooks, text books and video
games, to name a few. **Visual literacy** involves noticing detail and visual
clues in order to understand and interpret images. Visual clues include
content, colours, shapes, lines, light, as well as people, their facial
expressions and gestures.

Examples of integrating visual literacy into your everyday teaching
include when you use the image on the cover of a picturebook to **elicit**
children's ideas about a story, or play a memory game based on a
poster, or get children to spot the differences in photos of identical trees
to learn about the seasons. All these activities encourage children to
observe images in close detail and, with **probing questions**, contribute to
the development of visual literacy.

Another way to develop children's visual literacy is by getting them to
look at art. Start by using a **think aloud** activity to introduce children
to the idea of 'going for a walk' around a painting with their eyes. Ask
them to look at the top, bottom, middle, and what is close and far
away. Encourage them to notice and think about i) the scene and what's
happening, ii) the people and what they're thinking or feeling, iii) the
objects and colours, iv) the mood and atmosphere, v) how the painting
makes them feel, vi) how they think the artist wants them to feel, and
vii) whether or not they like the painting, and why.

Follow up by using projected images or sets of art postcards (see **78**)
and children look at and describe other paintings in the same way. You
may be surprised by the freshness and maturity of children's insights
and observations. You can also apply similar techniques to get children
to look critically at other still and moving visual images, such as
advertisements and video games.

By using multimodal texts, you develop children's ability to process content in different ways. This enhances their comprehension skills and appeals to children with different learning strengths and preferences.

Multimodal texts combine different modes of communication and are usual in most children's lives. In order for children to understand, interpret and think critically about multimodal texts, they need to be able to process the different modes that have been combined to communicate an overall message. Children frequently develop these skills in relation to storytelling and **content-based learning**.

Picturebooks combine illustrations, photos, text, colours, sizes and fonts in creative ways which contribute to readers' overall understanding and response. In some picturebooks, the illustrations and text tell the same story, whereas in others, they offer a dynamic contrast, which adds to the narrative suspense and children's enjoyment. Through effective questioning, you raise children's awareness of the ways the text and images interact. You can also get children to compare the oral/written text and images in print and animated versions and the way this influences their response.

In content-based learning, multimodal texts scaffold, or support, children's understanding of new concepts. For example, if children are learning about the water cycle, multimodal texts, such as an illustrated diagram combined with a written description or, for younger children, a water cycle song in an animated video, help children to understand the process. By using multimodal means to impart the same information, learning is made accessible, memorable and enjoyable.

You can also encourage older children to use technology to create their own multimodal texts, for example, for presentations (see **60**), class blog posts, videos, stories (see **89**), or content-based learning notes.

By laying the foundations of critical literacy, children develop a reflective, questioning attitude towards different forms of texts. You have a key role to play in this.

In a world of fake news, persuasive advertising and the manipulation of information online, it is more important than ever to lay the foundations of **critical literacy** in childhood. This helps children to detect the intentions, biases and motivations behind texts.

Critical literacy can be thought of as 'detecting the LIE', where L stands for Literal understanding, I stands for Interpretation and Inference, and E stands for Evaluation and Examination of features beyond the text such as the writer or composer, source and purpose.

The best way to encourage critical literacy is through gentle, **probing questions** which move children beyond the 'L' and get to the 'IE' (see also **49**). One way to approach this is to prepare relevant, **age-appropriate** *Wh-* questions which apply to the text children are working on.

Some examples of questions are:

Who is the author / composer of the text? Who is the text for?
What is the intention / purpose of the text? What do the words / images suggest? What in the text is fact / opinion? What does the author / composer want you to think / feel?
How are boys / girls / men / women / animals / different cultures / families / ages / races portrayed in the text? How does the text make you think / feel? How does the author / composer of the text achieve this?
Why was the text created? Why is the text interesting / useful?
When might the information / ideas be helpful?
Where can you find more information / evidence?

X: Grammar

Young children learn holistically and construct meaning from all available clues in their immediate environment. Through exposure to language in activities such as stories, songs, games and everyday classroom communication, they become familiar with grammatical patterns in formulaic sequences and unanalysed **chunks** of language. Through imitation, repetition, meaningful practice and recycling, children develop confidence in using language and transferring it to other contexts. The language children learn in this way also becomes an internal resource for later, more formal learning.

As children grow older and develop analytical skills, it becomes increasingly appropriate to encourage them to notice underlying grammatical patterns and forms. This develops their awareness and explicit understanding of grammar, as well as engages their curiosity in comparing English with their own language(s). It also enables children to begin to systematise their knowledge and potentially enriches and extends the ways in which they communicate.

A key question is when to move beyond implicit teaching–learning of language chunks and adopt a more explicit approach. There are no 'right answers' to this, and your decision depends on factors such as how long children have been learning English, their cognitive maturity and the approach used to teach their mother tongue. This will also influence your decision on whether or not it is helpful to introduce metalanguage, such as 'verb' or 'noun'.

My key tips for grammar are:

93 Make grammar child-friendly

94 Be a grammar detective!

95 Provide purposeful practice

96 Correct with a light touch

In order to make grammar child-friendly, children need to encounter the language in a relevant, meaningful context, such as a story, first. By using multi-sensory activities, you also make grammar memorable and enjoyable.

At times in your teaching, there may be a place for short grammatical explanations, possibly in the children's **shared language**. However, the most effective way of supporting children's emerging grammar is to give them hands-on opportunities to manipulate and experience grammar for themselves.

Some ideas for multi-sensory, child-friendly, grammar activities are:

- Spot the contractions: prepare word cards with sentences that are meaningful to children using full forms, e.g. *Leyla has got a carrot. / Yusef does not like peas.* In groups, children take a card and stand in a line to make their sentence. Children who have words which contract link arms, e.g. *does not = doesn't.* Other children check and read the sentence, first with the full form and then with contractions. From then on, use a gesture of linking arms whenever you wish to remind children to use contractions when they speak.

- Grammar colours: prepare colour-coded grammar cards based on the unit, topic or story, e.g. red for verbs, blue for nouns, green for adjectives, yellow for pronouns, etc. Use the cards to draw attention to relevant aspects of grammar, e.g. green words come before blue words, yellow words can replace blue words. You can also use the same colour system to get children to circle words you wish to focus on in a text, e.g. *Underline the verbs in red.*

- Deduce the question: invite two children to sit with their backs to the board. Write a question they can't see, e.g. *What do you like doing?* Other children prepare answers, e.g. *I like skateboarding.* The pair at the front invite children to say their sentences and deduce the question. The key to deducing the question is by paying attention to the grammar.

94 Be a grammar detective!

By getting children to be 'grammar detectives', they discover features of grammar themselves. This develops their language awareness and analytical skills and is likely to be more memorable than being told.

There is no guarantee that by discovering and noticing features of grammar, children will apply them to their own language **output**. However, such activities nevertheless play an invaluable role in extending and deepening children's understanding of grammar. They also prepare upper primary children for the transition to secondary school, where they are likely to be expected to learn grammar more formally.

Examples of activities which encourage children to notice grammar are:

- Be like Sherlock: establish a regular spot after work on texts or stories in which you get children to look back and find the answers to two or three specific 'grammar detective' questions, e.g. *Find two examples of 'some' and 'any'. When do we use 'some'? When do we use 'any'?*
- Discover the rules: give **input** and data about a grammar point. Children work in pairs and logically work out and 'discover' the rules, for example, for indefinite articles, e.g. *a banana, an orange*, etc. or for the formation of comparative adjectives, e.g. *tall – taller, pretty – prettier, dangerous – more dangerous*, etc.
- Apply the rules: reverse the above procedure and project the rules for a particular grammatical point, for example, the formation of plurals. Children then apply the rules and write the plurals of a set of familiar words in a table with the headings: *s / es / ies / irregular*.
- Stop!: children listen to a familiar story or text and call *Stop!* every time they hear the grammar point you want them to notice, for example, irregular past tense verbs.
- Clap the grammar: dictate a set of questions or sentences containing a target point of grammar, e.g. *can*. As you say each sentence or question, clap instead of saying *can* and children leave a space, e.g. *Ahmed (clap) speak Arabic. / (clap) you help me, please?* Children work in pairs to identify the missing word and the ways we use *can*, e.g. to talk about ability and make requests.

> By providing purposeful practice, children become familiar
> with using grammatical patterns and forms to express
> specific meanings. This develops their confidence and their
> ability to listen and interact with peers.

Although repetition has a place in getting children to manipulate
grammatical forms, it does not develop their ability to use them to
communicate. For this, you need to provide plenty of opportunities for
children to practise language in contextualised, supported frameworks
(see also **48**). There are many activities and games you can use that
also integrate the development of children's thinking skills, such as
recall or logical deduction, and social skills, such as turn-taking and
collaborating. Some versatile examples are:

- Information gap activities: an information gap is created by one
  child having information that another child doesn't know. By asking
  questions or exchanging information, the gap is closed. For example,
  if pairs of children each have partial information about a monster,
  they take turns to ask and answer questions, e.g. *How many eyes has
  it got?* to find out all the information.
- Guessing games: use these to practise questions and short form
  answers, e.g. *Is it …? Has it got …? Does it …?* There are many
  variations. For example, one child chooses an item in a picture, or an
  object in a 'feely bag' and others have ten questions to identify it.
- *Find someone who …*: use this for personalised grammar practice.
  Children move round the class asking and answering questions to
  find someone who, for example, likes broccoli, fish, etc. and write
  the names in the table. Reporting back on the completed tables
  provides additional practice of the third person too.

As well as activities such as the above, you also need to set up freer
situations in which children take risks and use all their language to
negotiate and express their own meaning (see **24, 31, 59, 67, 74, 83**).

96   Correct with a light touch

> It can be off-putting and demotivating for children to have their grammar constantly corrected. You need to think about what, when and how to correct, and use a light touch.

Whether in oral or written work, a rule of thumb is to respond to children's meaning rather than focus on their mistakes. Although children can benefit from corrective **feedback**, you need to balance this with considerations of their age and cognitive ability to analyse language as well as their confidence and enthusiasm to participate. You also need to take individual children's **learning differences** into account.

You can either do oral correction on the spot, as children speak, or as a follow-up later. Some options for on-the-spot oral correction are to **recast** what children want to say and re-express it correctly or to use gesture to indicate a mistake and children correct it themselves. You can also **elicit** correction by repeating what children say and pausing before the mistake to give time for self-correction or repeat the mistake with a puzzled look and questioning intonation to alert children to a mistake that they then self-correct. If necessary, you can correct explicitly by intervening to point out and correct a mistake.

With younger children, if you correct them at all, it's best to do so on the spot while the language is fresh in their minds. It's also more appropriate to use an approach such as recasting which gives children an opportunity to hear the correct version without drawing attention to the mistake.

With older children, you can either correct on the spot or later. The most important mistakes to correct are those which prevent communication from taking place. In the case of more open-ended activities, such as role plays or discussions, it's likely to be more appropriate not to interrupt the activity and to make a note of mistakes to go over afterwards. The most motivating oral correction techniques are those that give children an opportunity to self-correct. It's also important to convey that mistakes are a healthy part of learning and the most valuable thing is to learn from them.

Y: Assessment

Assessment involves using a range of different instruments in order to gather information and measure children's progress and performance over time. Some key questions are:

- Why assess? Assessment helps you to evaluate your teaching and take pedagogical decisions to make improvements. It also provides you with evidence to inform parents and children about their progress.
- When to assess? Assessment is an ongoing process. It includes everyday, **formative assessment, summative assessment** in the form of short assessment tasks or progress tests, and **peer** and **self-assessment**.
- Who assesses? As well as you, children play a role in peer and self-assessment and **assessment for learning** (AfL).
- How to assess? Assessment needs to be child-friendly and **age-appropriate**. It also needs to be ethical, accountable and support children's learning by providing a constructive and motivating experience. Assessment may include informal observation of children in class, end-of-unit and/ or end-of-term progress tests, **portfolios** and homework. With younger children, the emphasis is likely to be mainly, if not exclusively, on formative assessment during lessons. As children get older, assessment tends to include an increasing number of tests and, possibly, external exams.
- What to assess? This will be determined by language, content and skills that have been taught. It's also important to assess other factors such as children's participation and willingness to make an effort.

My key tips on assessment are:

- 97 Be wary of tests!
- 98 Integrate formative assessment
- 99 Give opportunities for peer and self-assessment
- 100 Involve children in assessment for learning (AfL)

---

97 Be wary of tests!

> You should never rely on tests as the only means of assessing children's progress. You also need to be wary of the suitability of tests and the possible negative effect they may have.

Progress tests provide a snapshot of how children are performing at one particular moment in time. This has an important formative function in giving both you and them **feedback** on learning that has taken place (see **100**). At the same time, tests can be stressful for children and, like everyone else, they have 'off days' which mean they may underperform. The test itself may also not be well-constructed or fit for purpose. For all these reasons, it's advisable that testing is just one of a range of instruments you use to gather evidence and information about children's progress over time.

When preparing progress tests for children, you need to think critically and ensure that the test is:

1. constructive and focuses on what children can do. This includes using task types that children are familiar with from everyday classroom practice, clear instructions and a marking system that reflects the test objectives and recognises children's achievement rather than penalises their mistakes;
2. valid and measures what it sets out to measure. For example, in a listening comprehension test, if written answers are required, the validity is questionable since it may not be clear whether children's listening or writing skills are being measured;
3. practical in terms of time, space and physical resources. For example, if a test includes a task where children listen and colour a picture, this may be time-consuming and pose class management problems. Children may also copy the colours their friends are using;
4. reliable in the sense that you have confidence that the test results will give you a consistent measure of children's progress;
5. likely to have a positive impact and washback effect in terms of enhancing children's **self-esteem** and sense of achievement as well as your methodology and teaching approach;
6. a support to the way in which you are accountable to the school, parents and children.

By integrating formative assessment as part of your everyday teaching, you build up a record of children's learning over time. This provides a balance and complements summative assessment and tests in evaluating children's progress.

Formative assessment is to do with gathering information and evidence about how children are learning and progressing during lessons. It is criterion-referenced, as opposed to norm-referenced, in that it measures children's progress in relation to specific learning standards, rather than ranking them in relation to their peers.

Formative assessment involves having a clear plan and clear criteria for aspects of learning you wish to assess. One of the major advantages of formative assessment is that it is not stressful for children and enables you to obtain evidence on aspects of learning that go beyond discrete linguistic items and skills.

An example of formative assessment is to regularly observe children as they carry out normal class activities and record their progress with reference to 'can do' statements on different areas of their learning.

Examples in relation to assessing children's oral communication skills might be: pronounces intelligibly; **recalls** vocabulary; responds to questions in context; participates in speaking; interacts with others; makes use of verbal and non-verbal strategies; uses classroom language.

Another way to carry out formative assessment is through evaluating samples of work that children build up during the year in a paper or electronic **portfolio**. By establishing, or negotiating, **success criteria** (see **14**) and getting children to select the pieces of work they wish to include in their portfolios, they participate actively in the assessment process. This develops their **metacognitive** skills and motivation to take decisions and plan how to improve (see also **100**).

99 Give opportunities for peer and self-assessment

> Through providing regular opportunities for peer and self-assessment, children develop metacognitive skills and their ability to interact empathetically with peers.

Young children's ability to consciously reflect and assess their learning is often underestimated. Here is an example of Jamie, a six-year-old English child, reflecting on his work after a story:

> a review of the story of nauty naughty
> teddy and the water
>
> my writing was good
>
> my ideas were OK
>
> But I cuold have made it longer
>
> my spelling I only got one mistake
>
> ✓ Good
>
> my drawing was neat

By getting children to evaluate their work, they learn to recognise their strengths and what they need to do to improve. This heightens their sense of responsibility for their learning (see also **100**).

Self-assessment usually takes place at the end of a unit of work following a **learning review** (see **19**). It typically includes either picture representations or a checklist of 'can do' statements. Alternative modes of self-assessment include getting children to draw a picture to show what they have learnt or to self-assess work in their **portfolios** (see **98**) or to keep a learner diary, possibly in their **shared language**.

Peer assessment engages children in interacting and giving **feedback** to classmates. This may be based on **success criteria** (see **14**) following project work, a presentation, a role play, or completing a self-assessment sheet for a partner and comparing views. An enjoyable peer assessment activity for younger pairs is to get them to take turns to role play being the teacher and use pictures to assess each other's vocabulary learning.

Involve children in assessment for learning (AfL)

By involving children in assessment for learning (AfL), you give them agency and a voice in the assessment process.

Assessment for learning (AfL) is an approach which integrates **formative assessment** into the fabric of everyday teaching and learning. The principal focus is on how to improve children's learning. Through techniques such as listening, observing, questioning, interacting with children and reviewing their work, you gather evidence which gives you insight into how well children are doing. This enables you to identify gaps, or needs, in their learning and establish suitable learning objectives. It also enables you to give children **feedback** which helps them to set personal learning goals and identify the next steps to improve.

AfL develops most effectively in a warm and supportive learning environment where children feel valued and engage in frequent, regular dialogue about their learning. Throughout this book, there are a number of tips you can draw on to implement AfL. These include:

- giving children feedback and praise in a way that constructively informs them about their learning (see **11** and **32**);
- using evidence you gather from interaction with children to negotiate and establish learning **outcomes** and **success criteria** (see **14**);
- conducting regular **learning reviews** (see **18** and **19**);
- building a positive relationship with children (see **5**) and promoting social and emotional skills and attitudes, such as cooperation, effort, resilience (see **32**), **autonomy** and responsible decision-making (see **8**);
- using questioning techniques to find out what children know and to support them in deciding what they need to do next to improve (see **49**);
- using observation to gather evidence on children's learning (see **98**);
- involving children in **peer** and **self-assessment** (see **99**);
- making use of tests in a formative, non-judgemental way (see **97**).

By consciously making AfL part of your practice, you're likely to notice a positive impact on children's motivation and learning.

Z: The last word

Whatever your teaching context, there are likely to be aspects over which you have no control and cannot change. These may include, for example, the number of children in your classes, the size and layout of your classroom, or the syllabus you are obliged to follow.

It is all too easy to fall into the trap of spending a lot of time and negative energy on such constraints. However, the key to effective and rewarding primary language teaching is to positively focus your multiple skills and energy on all the things over which you do have control and influence. These include the care and interest you show in individual children's motivation, learning and achievement, and the efforts you make to prepare and deliver dynamic, varied and suitably challenging lessons. They also include the way you value children's **diversity** and unique potential to learn, and your skills in relating to children and teaching them in a way that will make a difference to their lives.

Positive beliefs, in whatever teaching circumstances, underpin your attitude and effectiveness as a teacher. In turn, these positive beliefs also influence the motivation, enjoyment and success of children as learners.

Positive beliefs include being constantly open to ideas and willing to learn from your experience, reading and other sources. I know, for example, that every time I come out of a primary classroom, whether I've been observing a lesson or teaching it myself, I almost always learn something new – whether in relation to the children, the materials, the procedures, or myself. A commitment to being a primary language teacher is, therefore, also a commitment to life-long learning as well.

My key tip for the last word is:
101 Believe in yourself and your children – and keep on learning!

Believe in yourself and your children – and keep on learning!

> If you believe in yourself as a teacher, and are convinced that you make a difference to the lives and learning of the children you teach, this is likely to impact positively on how effective you are in the classroom. You also need to have a mindset in which you never stop learning.

In order to sustain a belief in yourself as a teacher over time, it's essential to look after your physical and mental wellbeing. This means doing what you can to stay healthy, building positive relationships with colleagues and finding time to switch off.

It also helps to develop an outlook in which you consciously look for the positive in things. For example, at the end of the teaching day, try the activity suggested for children (see **57**) and think of three things that went well, rather than focusing on things that went wrong. In the same way that you foster a growth mindset in children (see **32**), work on your own mindset by continuously learning and experimenting rather than always repeating the same lessons in the same way.

Your wellbeing has a significant influence on children's wellbeing. If you also believe in your children as learners, and have high expectations of what they can achieve, this is likely to positively impact their learning, attitudes and self-beliefs. As a recent, popular meme by a six-year-old child goes: 'My teacher thought I was smarter than I was – so I was'.

In order to keep on learning, there are multiple possibilities including collaborating with colleagues, reading (you might like to start with the Selected further reading on page 135), attending conferences and webinars, joining social media groups with a professional focus and becoming a member of a teachers' association.

Whatever you do to continue your professional development, always remember your invaluable role in developing children's learning potential and confidence as speakers of English – and best of luck!

Glossary

affective climate: the emotional atmosphere of the classroom (see **10, 16, E Introduction, 44**)

age-appropriate: reflects children's interests and stages of cognitive, emotional, psychological, social and physical development (see **3, 11, 34, 92, Y Introduction**)

agency: active role and voice in decisions and actions (see **8, 37, 50, 54, 100**)

assessment for learning (AfL): process of gathering and interpreting evidence of learning by teachers and children in order to adjust teaching and learning strategies and set suitable learning goals (see **18, Y Introduction, 100**)

autonomy: acting in a self-regulated and self-directed way (see **3, 8, E Introduction J Introduction, 37, O Introduction, 57, 77, 83, 86, 100**)

behaviour plan: a guide to strategies and procedures to support classroom management (see **4**)

chunk: connected words or formulaic language that children learn as a single concept (see **31, I Introduction, 51, N Introduction, 54, T Introduction, U Introduction, 82, X Introduction**)

class contract: an agreed set of rules and norms for classroom procedures and behaviour (see **3**)

classroom routines: procedures that you use regularly and repeatedly for carrying out everyday classroom activities (see **3, 4, 71, U Introduction**)

cognitive development: emerging ability to think, perceive and understand the world in more complex and mature ways (see **6, H Introduction, 52, W Introduction**)

cognitive skills: abilities that involve memory and thought processes such as analysing, comparing, classifying and linking cause and effect (see **M Introduction, 71, 80**)

communication strategies: ways of conveying intended meaning, either non-verbally, e.g. by facial expression or gesture, or verbally, e.g. by describing or re-phrasing (see **M Introduction**)

content-based learning: a focus on real world knowledge or subjects from other areas of the curriculum, such as geography or art (see **24, 34, L Introduction, 46, 78, 91**)

cooperative learning: teaching strategy in which children work together in pairs or groups in order to share ideas, support and learn from each other and produce a collective outcome (see **B Introduction, 5, 7, 45, O Introduction, 57, 75, 78**)

critical literacy: ability to analyse texts in a questioning way in order to understand the intentions, biases and motivations that lie behind them (see **85, W Introduction, 92**)

critical thinking: ability to question, analyse and reflect on ideas, issues or problems in order to form opinions and judgements (see **M Introduction, Q Introduction, 86**)

cumulative: describes a language pattern which is repeated and successively added to, as in some stories and games (see **7, 21, 82**)

decode: match letters and sounds in order to be able to recognise written words (see **N Introduction, 85**)

differentiate: make learning appropriate for individual children depending on their needs (see **22, 39, 71, 72, 79**)

digital literacy: ability to access information and to communicate, collaborate and create content using digital technologies (see **89**)

discovery techniques: experiential hands-on or problem-solving activities which lead children to new learning (see **47**)

diversity: individual differences among children including race, ethnicity, gender, ability, age, nationality, culture, religion, languages, personality, learning strengths and preferences (see **F Introduction, 21, 22, K Introduction, R Introduction, 70, 77, Z Introduction**)

elicit: use oral or visual prompts, questions, actions or gestures to encourage children to contribute what they know (see **6, 22, 23, 40, 53, 74, 88, 90, 96**)

engagement: interest, attention and willingness to learn in a sustained way (see **2, 13, 15, 22, 41, 44, S Introduction**)

exclusion: state of being rejected and not accepted socially (see **F Introduction, 24, 31**)

feedback: information given to children about their learning (see **4, 11, 38, 49, 57, 66, 67, 71, S Introduction, U Introduction, 96, 97, 99, 100**)

formative assessment: process of gathering information and evidence about the progress of learners over time (see **Y Introduction, 98, 100**)

functional language: language used for specific communicative purposes such as agreeing and disagreeing in a role play or debate (see **24, 31, 60, 64, 67, 83**)

global issues: problems that impact the whole world such as climate change, poverty, social justice or gender equality (see **21, 24**)

graphic organiser: a visual way of organising and presenting information (see **47, 52, 72**)

higher-order thinking skills: cognitive processes, such as analysing and evaluating, that contrast with lower-order thinking skills, such as remembering and understanding (see **24, 46**)

inclusive: involves everyone, without prejudice or discrimination, and gives a sense of emotional security and belonging (see **5, 44, R Introduction, 69, 71, T Introduction**)

input: exposure to language and content through multimodal sources (see **6, 15, 16, 67, 72, T Introduction, U Introduction, 94**)

intercultural competence: knowledge, skills, attitudes and awareness that underpin respect for, and effective communication with, people from other cultures (see **24, K Introduction, 43, 44, O Introduction**)

language repertoire: all the language(s) children currently know and have available to use (see **M Introduction, 83**)

learning cycle: stages of learning organised cyclically and based on experience and reflection (see **16, 22, 80**)

learning differences: individual variation in aspects such as cognition, learning, sensory and physical skills, social, emotional and behavioural skills, communication and interaction (see **56, 71, T Introduction, 77, 96**)

learning preferences: preferred ways of learning, for example, using images or movement, or on your own or with others (see **15, 17, 55, 69, 70, 71, 72**)

learning review: procedure which guides children in reflecting on their learning in order to lead to improved outcomes (see **7, 13, 17, 18, 19, 28, 38, 44, 50, 63, 77, U Introduction, 99, 100**)

learning strategy: plan of action to achieve a specific learning goal (see **E Introduction, 17, 18, 55**)

life skills: wide range of personal, social and thinking skills that develop children's practical ability to deal positively with everyday life (see **O Introduction, 58, T Introduction, 80**)

lockstep: describes a teacher-led approach in which the whole class does the same thing in the same way at the same time (see **8**)

mediator: person who shows sensitivity and insight in adjusting teaching strategies to make learning effective for individual differences and needs (see **E Introduction**)

metacognitive: describes thought processes used to plan, monitor and evaluate learning (see **16, E Introduction, 17, M Introduction, 49, 50, 52, 55, 77, 98, 99**)

model: explicitly demonstrate a procedure in order to provide a clear example for learners to follow (see **3, 5, 6, 16, 17, 27, 38, 47, 51, 52, P Introduction, 62, Q Introduction, S Introduction, 73, 74, 81, 85, 86**)

monitor: closely observe childen's actions, language, progress and behaviour (see **7, E Introduction, 28, J Introduction, 38, P Introduction, 62, 89**)

multilingual identities: qualities, beliefs and personalities shaped by exposure to multiple languages and cultures at home and at school (see **5, 44, 71**)

multimodal texts: information or content presented in a way that combines different modes of communication such as print, images, graphics, audio, film and music (see **W Introduction, 91**)

multi-sensory activities: procedures and games that engage children in using two or more senses at the same time (see **16, 93**)

off task: not engaged or focused on the work or activity which has been set up (see **11, 12, J Introduction, 39**)

on task: engaged and focused on the work or activity which has been set up (see **12, 39**)

outcome: what children achieve and are able to do by the end of an activity, lesson or unit of work (see **A Introduction, 8, D Introduction, 14, 16, 18, 19, 22, 23, 27, H Introduction, J Introduction, 38, 39, 45, M Introduction, 50, 51, P Introduction, 68, 71, S Introduction, 74, 79, 80, 100**)

output: what children produce as a result of learning (see **72, 94**)

parameters of behaviour: limits or boundaries of classroom behaviour that you are willing to allow or tolerate (see **A Introduction, 4, C Introduction, 10**)

peer assessment: process of giving feedback and evaluating the work of classmates (see **18, 60, Y Introduction, 99, 100**)

phonics: method of teaching sound–spelling relationships by decoding letters into sounds (see **56, 84, V Introduction**)

portfolio: a personalised profile and record of language experience including samples of work which show, and can be used to assess, progress (see **18, 20, Y Introduction, 98, 99**)

probing questions: questions that lead to thinking more deeply (see **49, 90, 92**)

recall: deliberately remember (see **19, 50, N Introduction, 55, 82, 95, 98**)

recast: re-express what children say in language that is correct (see **6, 22, 24, 44, 74, 96**)

recycle: use previously introduced language or vocabulary in different contexts or with different skills in order to extend learning (see **54**)

reward system: way to acknowledge and recognise achievement and/or positive behaviour (see **4, 86**)

scaffolding: strategies and techniques which facilitate and support children's learning (see **22, 47, 83**)

self-assessment: process of evaluating your own learning (see **16, 18, Y Introduction, 99, 100**)

self-esteem: positive self-regard and confidence in your own worth and abilities (see **2, 5, 10, 11, 16, 30, 32, I Introduction, 40, 44, O Introduction, P Introduction, U Introduction, 97**)

shared language: language that children are being educated in, which may or may not be their mother tongue (see **6, 14, E Introduction, 19, 22, 25, 28, 30, 39, 47, 49, 53, 66, 74, 93**)

stir and settle: the principle of following a lively activity with one that calms children down (see **9, Q Introduction**)

substitution table: a grid giving options to make sentences following a set pattern (see **31, 47**)

success criteria: features which provide evidence that a learning outcome has been achieved (see **14, 17, 18, 19, 38, 71, 72, 79, 80, 88, 98, 99, 100**)

summative assessment: method of evaluation to measure children's achievement at the end of a unit or period of instruction (see **Y Introduction, 98**)

think aloud: technique in which the process of how to solve a problem or carry out an activity is explicitly verbalised (see **6, 17, 47, 90**)

think-pair-share: technique in which learners think individually and discuss in pairs before exchanging their ideas with a larger group (see **7, 82**)

translanguaging: process whereby bilingual or multilingual learners mix and use all their languages to communicate (see **24, 44, U Introduction**)

values: core attitudes and beliefs that underline and influence the way we think and act in different situations (see **5, 21, 24, H Introduction, 29, 30, 31, J Introduction, 41, 45, O Introduction, 59, 67, 69, 72, T Introduction, 77, 80**)

visual literacy: the ability to interpret and understand images (see **78, 86, 90**)

Zone of Proximal Development (ZPD): the area of potential learning in which a child can carry out an activity with appropriate support from a more knowledgeable or skilled adult or peer (see **T Introduction**)

Selected further reading

Bentley, K. (2009) *Primary Curriculum Box: CLIL Lessons and Activities for Younger Learners*. Cambridge: Cambridge University Press.

Bland, J. (Ed.) (2015) *Teaching English to Young Learners. Critical Issues in Language Teaching with 3–12 year olds*. London: Bloomsbury Academic.

Cameron, L. (2001) *Teaching Languages to Young Learners*. Cambridge: Cambridge University Press.

Douglas, S. (Ed.) (2019) *Creating an Inclusive School Environment*. London: British Council.

Ellis, G. and Brewster, J. (2014) *Tell it Again! The Storytelling Handbook for Primary English Language Teachers* (3rd edition). London: British Council.

Ellis, G. and Ibrahim, N. (2015) *Teaching children how to learn*. Delta Publishing.

Enever, J. (Ed.) (2011) *ELLiE. Early Language Learning in Europe*. London: British Council.

Enever, J., Moon, J. and Raman, U. (Eds.) (2009) *Young Learner English Language Policy and Implementation: International Perspectives*. Reading: Garnet.

Garton, S. and Copland, F. (Eds.) (2019) *Handbook of Teaching English to Young Learners*. New York, NY: Routledge.

Giannikas, C., McLaughlin, L., Fanning, G. and Deutsch Muller, N. (Eds.) (2015) *Children Learning English: From Research to Practice*. Reading: Garnet Publishing.

Mackay, P. and Guse, J. (2007) *Five-Minute Activities for Young Learners*. Cambridge: Cambridge University Press.

Maley, A. and Peachey, N. (Eds.) (2015) *Integrating Global Issues in the Creative English Language Classroom*. London: British Council.

Maley, A. and Peachey, N. (Eds.) (2017) *Creativity in Language*

Teaching. London: British Council.

Moon, J. (2000) *Children Learning English*. Oxford: Macmillan Education.

Murphy, V. (2014) *Second Language Learning in the Early School Years: Trends and Contexts*. Oxford: Oxford University Press.

Pilar García Mayo, M. del. (2017) *Learning Foreign Languages in Primary School*. Bristol: Multilingual Matters.

Pinter, A. (2011) *Children Learning Second Languages*. Basingstoke: Palgrave Macmillan.

Pinter, A. (2017) *Teaching Young Language Learners* (2nd edition). Oxford: Oxford University Press.

Prosic-Santovac, D. and Rixon, S. (2019) *Integrating Assessment into Early Language Teaching and Learning*. Bristol: Multilingual Matters.

Puchta, H. and Williams, M. (2012) *Teaching Young Learners to Think: ELT Activities for Young Learners Aged 6–12*. Helbling Publishers.

Read, C. (2007) *500 Activities for the Primary Classroom*. Oxford: Macmillan Education.

Rixon, S. (2013) *British Council Survey of Policy and Practice in Primary English Language Teaching Worldwide*. London: British Council.

Shin, J. K. and Crandall, J. A. (2014) *Teaching Young Learners English: From Theory to Practice*. Boston, MA: National Geographic Learning / Cengage Learning.

Wagner, M., Conlon Perugini, D. and Byram, M. (Eds.) (2018) *Teaching Intercultural Competence Across the Age Range: From Theory to Practice*. Bristol: Multilingual Matters.

Index